Old Capitol

A Bur Oak Original

Old Capitol

Portrait of an Iowa Landmark

By Margaret N. Keyes

University of Iowa Press

Iowa City

University of Iowa Press, Iowa City 52242

Copyright © 1988 by the University of Iowa

All rights reserved

Printed in the United States of America

First edition, 1988

Design by Richard Hendel

Typesetting by G & S Typesetters, Austin, Texas

Printing and binding by Edwards Brothers, Ann Arbor, Michigan

Library of Congress Cataloging-in-Publication Data

Keyes, Margaret N., 1918–
Old Capitol: portrait of an Iowa landmark/by Margaret N. Keyes.—1st ed.
    p.   cm.—(A Bur oak original)
Bibliography: p.
Includes index.
ISBN 0-87745-210-5
1. Old Capitol (Iowa City, Iowa)—Conservation and restoration. 2. Architecture, Modern—19th century—Iowa—Iowa City—Conservation and restoration. 3. Historic buildings—Iowa—Iowa City—Conservation and restoration. 4. Iowa City (Iowa)—Buildings, structures, etc.—Conservation and restoration. 5. University of Iowa—Buildings—Conservation and restoration. I. Title. II. Series.
NA4413.I84K4   1988
727'.3'028809777—dc19   88-22689
                                                              CIP

Frontispiece: East facade. Photo University Photo Service, c. 1950.

To Willard L. Boyd,
*who envisioned not only
the restoration of Old Capitol
but also this historical record
of the building*

Contents

Acknowledgments / xi

Introduction / xiii

1. The Territorial and Statehood Years, 1842–1857 / 1

2. The University Years, 1857–1970 / 22

3. The Rehabilitation, 1921–1924 / 46

4. The Architectural Restoration, 1970–1976 / 73

5. The Interior / 94

6. The Dedication / 121

Epilogue / 130

Appendix A. Old Capitol Restoration Committee / 139

Appendix B. University Student Involvement / 142

Appendix C. Old Capitol Dedication Program / 143

Notes / 145

Select Bibliography / 151

Index / 165

Acknowledgments

One of the meaningful benefits of the research process is the privilege of first contacting and then learning to know and appreciate many individuals. In researching the history, construction, and furnishings of Iowa's first state capitol and in restoring the building, I have worked with numerous people. Each of them has left an imprint on the final outcome of my work, this manuscript. I contacted so many between 1970 and 1988, and I regret that not all may be named here. Many will find their names included in the text in connection with their specific contributions, others will find themselves credited in the appendixes, and still others will know only that I am aware of what they did—and that I am most appreciative.

The restoration of Old Capitol was initiated by Willard L. Boyd, president of the University of Iowa, in the summer of 1970. By appointing me director of research for the project, he involved me in a fascinating academic pursuit that resulted in a new career direction in the ensuing years. I extend to him my most sincere thanks for the challenge he presented and for his support throughout the project.

I am also indebted to many others for their efforts and cooperation throughout the long process: the members of the Old Capitol Restoration Committee, especially its chair, Susan Hancher; the University students who served as graduate research assistants; the University faculty and staff; the off-campus architects and other professionals, all of whom served as advisors; and finally, the workers who re-created the building and its furnishings. All these people are now a significant part of the history of Old Capitol.

The late Fred W. Kent, whose legacy to Johnson County, Iowa City, and the University is to be found in extensive photograph files in the University Archives, served on the restoration committee and provided all the historic photographs of Old Capitol in this manuscript that are not otherwise credited. The recent interior photographs of the restored building are the work of Don Roberts of the University Photo Service.

Earl M. Rogers, archivist of the Special Collections Division, University of Iowa Libraries, supplied information, photographs, and unlimited patience. Among the many librarians who have been of inestimable help in the exploration of Old Capitol's history are Mary Bennett, manuscripts librarian of the State Historical Society of Iowa in Iowa City, and Lida Lisle Green, history librarian of the State Historical Society of Iowa in Des Moines. Leeta M. Berry, library assistant at the University of Iowa Libraries, provided her expertise and helped us conserve many of the original books in the territorial–state library.

Without the interest and cooperation of all levels of the central administration of the University of Iowa, the restoration could not have been undertaken. I especially appreciate the support and encouragement of Floy Eugenia Whitehead and Sara C. Wolfson, both former chairs of the Department of Home Economics, who made my leaves-of-absence possible.

Darrell D. Wyrick, president of the University of Iowa Foundation, and his fellow directors were untiring in their efforts to secure more than half the funding for the 1970s restoration, and they have continued to supply support and advice. I thank them especially for funding a semester's leave-of-absence in 1982–1983 and for supporting my work on this monograph.

The contribution of Bette A. Thompson to this venture is difficult to describe. I can only say that during fifteen years of daily association on behalf of Old Capitol I have been constantly aware of her concern, support, understanding, and friendship, and I thank her most sincerely. I also extend deep appreciation to Ann M. Smothers and to the entire staff and all volunteers at Old Capitol.

Introduction

Territory of Iowa Capitol, Iowa State Capitol, Iowa State House, Stone Hall, Central Hall, University Hall, Middle Building, Cradle of Iowa, Pride of the Pentacrest, Old Stone Capitol—each has been used at some time in the past 147 years to designate the building today known as Old Capitol. Together they identify the many uses that the building has served. They also indicate the affection and respect that friends of Old Capitol feel for the venerable structure.

When Willard L. Boyd, fifteenth president of the University of Iowa, announced on July 18, 1970, that Old Capitol was to be restored, he established the basis for preserving its many functions and for enhancing its sentimental and esthetic value. He appointed Susan Hancher, wife of the late Virgil M. Hancher, thirteenth president of the University, to chair the Old Capitol Restoration Committee. Frank T. Nye, University alumnus and associate editor of the *Cedar Rapids Gazette*, agreed to be the vice-chair, and I became director of research for the project, thus adding to my duties as a professor in the Department of Home Economics. Joseph W. Meyer, executive director of the alumni association, and Darrell D. Wyrick, then executive director of the University of Iowa Foundation, helped us form a thirty-five-member national committee of University students, faculty, administration, alumni, and friends to determine policies and procedures for the restoration.

The Old Capitol Restoration Committee met for the first time on October 3, 1970, in what was then called the board room, the large, northwest-corner room on the first floor of Old Capitol. We made two decisions that guided the entire restoration process. One was that the restoration would reflect the total history of Old Capitol, including the territorial, state, and University occupancies of the building. The second decision was that Old Capitol would be a "living museum"; it would provide space not just for look-but-don't-touch exhibits but also for continuing University traditions and other appropriate functions.

Six years later in 1976, the restored Old Capitol was opened to the public as a major event in the University's recognition of the United States of America Bicentennial. More than six thousand people attended the dedication, and twelve thousand toured Old Capitol during the bicentennial weekend, July 3–5.

Old Capitol

1. The Territorial and Statehood Years, 1842–1857

Not many miles from where Old Capitol stands above the Iowa River, an original Iowan, a native American, attended a gathering of Johnson County pioneers on July 4, 1838. They were celebrating the establishment of the Iowa Territory, but Chief Poweshiek was thinking of his people's loss. He spoke to the new Iowans:

> Soon I shall go to a new home and you will plant corn where my dead sleep. Our towns, the paths we have made, and the flowers we love will soon be yours. I have moved many times and have seen the white man put his feet in the tracks of the Indian and make the earth into fields and gardens. I know that I must go away and you will be so glad when I am gone that you will soon forget that the meat and the lodge-fire of the Indian have been forever free to the stranger and at all times he has asked for what he has fought for, the right to be free.[1]

The future they would create was clearly in Poweshiek's thinking, but he could not have envisioned the capitol building to be constructed nearby and the varied role it would play in the future of Iowa.

Just six months later on January 1, 1839, the Iowa territorial legislature passed an act authorizing the formation of a commission to locate the permanent seat of government for the territory "at the most eligible point within the present limits of Johnson County."[2]

Chauncey Swan, John Ronalds, and Robert Ralston were elected to serve as commissioners. On May 1, 1839, Swan and Ronalds met at the village of Napoleon near the site of Poweshiek's settlement to begin exploration of the Iowa River area in Johnson County. Three days later on May 4, 1839, Ralston joined them, and they officially located the new capital, already designated Iowa City by the legislature, on the east bank of the Iowa River, about two miles north of Napoleon near the geographical center of Johnson County. The three commissioners also marked the site of the capitol building by driving into the ground a wooden stake that bore the carved legend, "Seat of Government, City of Iowa, May 4th, 1839, C. Swan, John Ronalds, Robt. Ralston, Commissioners."[3] The availability of building materials was of prime importance, and they had agreed that nearby forests of hickory and oak, quarries of limestone and sandstone, and clay suited to making bricks were all of the best quality.

Chauncey Swan continued to serve the territory as acting commissioner of the new seat of government and directed the survey that platted the new town. First he determined the dimensions for Capitol Square, which surrounded the site for the statehouse. Then he planned the streets, alleys, market places, church sites, Governor's Square, and a promenade along the Iowa River with the statehouse as the focal point.

Plans for the capitol building were also developed under Swan's direction. A notice dated May 4, 1839, and later printed in at least two Iowa newspapers invited bids for materials to be used in constructing public buildings in Iowa City.[4] The building specifications in the notice clearly were not written by an experienced architect, and the dimensions do not match those of the statehouse that was finally constructed. Although the commissioners stated that "a plan of the building and bills may be seen by application," the structure described—"a main building . . . with two wings" and "12 columns"—was not the plan actually adopted. No later references to such a plan appear to exist, except for a drawing on a draft of an 1839 Iowa City map. A second 1839 map, however, considered by historians to be the earliest Iowa City map in existence, has no drawing of a proposed capitol (fig. 1).

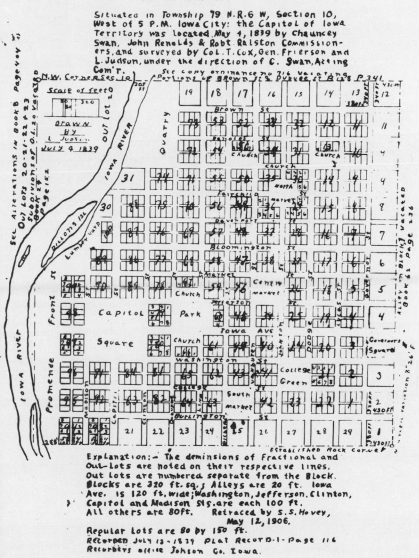

1. *Original map of Iowa City, 1839.*

2. *Masthead of the* Iowa Standard, *January 12, 1843. First used December 8, 1842. Designed by Charles A. Robbins, Iowa City.*

The earliest known drawing of the building that was constructed appeared in an 1843 masthead of the *Iowa Standard,* the first newspaper published in Iowa City. It shows the basic form and some details of the structure but is poorly proportioned, particularly the cupola (fig. 2). It may have been drawn from a verbal description only, since construction of the building had not progressed enough by 1843 to permit firsthand knowledge of the cupola and the entrance.

Architect

The first recorded contact between architect John Francis Rague of Springfield, Illinois, and an official of the Iowa Territory occurred on November 12, 1839. On that date Chauncey Swan and Rague drew up a contract naming Rague contractor for the Iowa capitol. It stated that Rague would be in charge of erecting the structure "to the top of the horizontal cornice, porticos, columns, entablatures, &c., in two years from that date, according to the original plans." [5] Clearly, building plans must have existed then for the Greek Revival structure that was built, or at least for a very similar one. Yet the actual contract has not been located, nor has any record of an earlier meeting between Swan and Rague been found. The construction contract was made out to "Rague and Co.," according to information in legislative journals. The "company" included two of Rague's associates, William Skeen [Skean?] and William McDonald. Both men had worked with Rague on the Illinois capitol, and he persuaded them to join him as partners in the construction of the Iowa statehouse.

Rague's name as architect entered the official records of the Iowa Territory on December 6, 1839, when Chauncey Swan reported to the legislature that "a draft of the plan for the erection of the public buildings is in the hands of the Architect, Mr. Rague, of Springfield, Illinois."[6] Additional references to Rague as architect of the statehouse occur in other legislative journals and appear to substantiate that he was, indeed, the architect of the building.

And yet, a legend has developed that a Roman Catholic priest, Samuel Charles Mazzuchelli, was Old Capitol's architect. The legend claims that if Mazzuchelli did not design the entire building he at least designed the spiral staircase, the cupola, or both. No documentation from primary sources has been found to support either idea, although Benjamin F. Shambaugh's 1939 publication, *The Old Stone Capitol Remembers*, gives sympathetic treatment to "The Mazzuchelli Legend." Shambaugh evaluated numerous questions about the priest's possible connection with the building and investigated all available leads, as did researchers of the 1970s involved with the building's restoration. Both he and they concluded that no documentary evidence is available to connect Father Mazzuchelli with the design of Old Capitol.[7]

There are, however, three references in primary sources to Mazzuchelli's contact with the early territorial government. The first, dated May 29, 1839 (just twenty-five days after the capitol site was determined), states that a sample of "elegant grey marble" from the quarries to be used in building the capitol was shown to Father Mazzuchelli.[8] No reason is given, but the priest may well have been an expert in judging quality of stone as a result of architectural study in his native Italy. Samples of the stone were also shown to other people in the area for their evaluation.

The second Mazzuchelli reference concerns the use of a room in St. Paul's Catholic Church in Burlington by the Council (Senate) of the Third Legislative Assembly of the Territory of Iowa, beginning on November 17, 1840. A listing of territorial expenses, dated March 5, 1841, states that voucher number eighty-three provided for the payment of $300 to Mazzuchelli for "rent of room occupied by Council."[9] Mazzuchelli's third contact with the territorial government was also in 1841, when he was paid $60 for rent of a room used "to store the furniture of the Legislature and Council for 12 months."[10]

These primary source references concerning a business relationship between Mazzuchelli and officials of the territorial government are the only ones that have been located. A brief statement in the priest's *Memoirs* indicates merely that he had observed the capitol in its early days of construction. It gives no more information concerning the building than a casual observer at the site might have offered.[11]

A personal letter of John F. Rague, on the other hand, adds strong support to the legislative documentation of his authorship of the capitol plans. An 1856 letter from Rague to P. [Phineas] M. Casady was found in the Casady files at the Iowa Historical Museum and Archives in Des Moines in 1971 by a librarian who was researching an unrelated topic. Realizing the significance of the letter, he shared his discovery with the researchers for the 1970s restoration (fig. 3).

In the letter Rague asserts, "I made the plans and Erected the Capitol at Springfield Illinois, and about the same time I made the plans for the Iowa Capitol." Indeed, the strong similarity of the Iowa statehouse to the Illinois capitol, which Rague designed in 1837, supports his assertion (fig. 4).

Rague's qualifying statement—"although I do not speak of the latter Building [Iowa Capitol] with any Degree of pride inasmuch as the plans were not carried out"—probably means that the plans were not carried out as he intended. In fact, Rague resigned as

Dubuque Iowa May 15th 56

Mr P. M. Casady

Dr Sir

*Your Homestead Informs me that
I might take the priviledges
of writting to You, for information
in regard to the Capitol to be
erected at Your place, my object
in doing So, is that I Should be
pleased to make the plans for it
In about 1839 I made the plans
and Erected the Capital at Springfield
Illinois, and about the Same time I
made the plans for the Iowa Capitol
although I do not Speak of the latter
Building with any Degree of pride
inasmuch as the plans were not
Carried out, any information you
may be pleased to give me will be Appreciated*

Respy
John. F. Rague
Architect Dubuque
Iowa

3. Letter from John F. Rague to P. M. Casady, May 15, 1856.
Courtesy State Historical Society of Iowa, Des Moines.

4. *Old State Capitol, Springfield, Illinois, c. 1866.*
Courtesy Wayne C. Temple, Illinois State Archives, Springfield.

contractor for the construction of the Iowa building on July 13, 1840.[12] An editorial in the *Burlington Hawk-Eye and Iowa Patriot* on July 23, 1840, states:

> We have been informed by Mr. Rague, Architect and Con-
> tractor of the Iowa Capitol, that on account of failure of the
> Quarry, the commissioners and himself have amicably can-

celled the contract, and Mr. R. is employed by the Commissioners to make all the detail drawing as the work progresses. We understand the original plan of the building will be preserved.[13]

Rague was evidently dissatisfied with the quality and amount of limestone, frequently but incorrectly called "marble" or "bird's-eye marble." Additional references suggest that he also considered the funding for the building inadequate. Certain design elements of the plan, such as a decorative entablature on the exterior, had had to be eliminated and these were "not carried out."

All in all, various sources document the fact that John F. Rague was the architect of Old Capitol. In addition, a scroll was reportedly placed in the capitol cornerstone on the day it was laid, July 4, 1840, with this notation: "John F. Rague, Architect of the Capitol of Iowa." The Mazzuchelli legend may have charm and is intriguing to pursue, but the primary source documentation that firmly establishes Rague as the architect of the building cannot be denied.

Construction

At the time Rague resigned as contractor, the building foundation reached only to the level immediately above the cornerstone. Rague was paid $150, and his plans for the structure were turned over to Chauncey Swan, who then became superintendent of public buildings. Since the original plans have never been located, we cannot be sure to what extent they were modified. We can assume, though, that the plans transferred from Rague to Swan were generally followed. Although smaller, the resulting building is very similar in plan and appearance to Rague's design for the Illinois capitol. Moreover, an 1840 legislative committee report lists information that describes Old Capitol as it exists today. Identifying characteristics include the dimensions—"one hundred and twenty feet long north and south and sixty feet east and west"—and other features—"foundation walls six feet thick" and "eight pilasters,

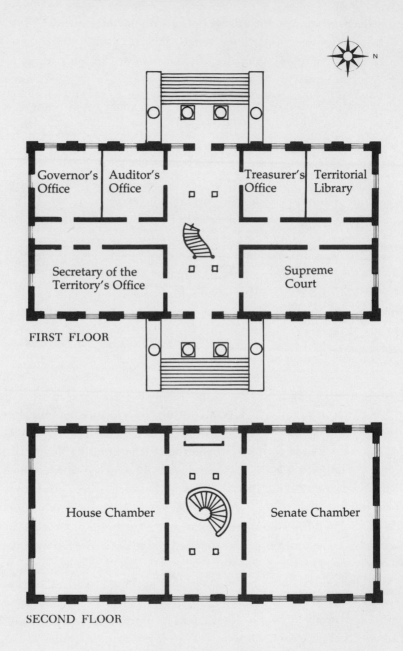

FIRST FLOOR

Governor's Office	Auditor's Office
Treasurer's Office	Territorial Library
Secretary of the Territory's Office	Supreme Court

SECOND FLOOR

House Chamber	Senate Chamber

5. *Original floor plans of Old Capitol.*

four feet wide, and projecting ten inches" on each of the fronts.[14] The interior floor plan described in the report was also followed (fig. 5).

Specifications for materials included limestone for the exterior walls. The first source of this stone was a quarry at the north end of Clinton Street, five to six blocks from the capitol behind the area where the University president's residence now stands. The stone from that quarry is properly described as the Coralville member of the Cedar Valley limestone of the Devonian period. Despite Rague's dissatisfaction with the stone, work in that quarry must have been very active in the early days of construction. The 1841 payrolls list fifty-six quarry labourers, drillers, and haulers as well as forty stonecutters.

On December 13, 1841, Swan reported to the legislature that the east wall of the capitol had been raised thirty-five feet above the ground to the point where the cornice was to begin, while the other walls were thirty feet high. To protect the building through the winter months when work could not continue, a temporary roof had been constructed.

Swan's last official act as superintendent of buildings was to inform the House of Representatives on January 5, 1842, that $33,330 would be needed to complete the building. Initial construction funds had included $20,000 granted the territory by the United States government and $19,000 raised by the sale of lots in Iowa City. This total of $39,000 had also covered Rague's work as architect and contractor.

Swan's tenure as both acting commissioner and superintendent of public buildings was under scrutiny by the legislature from time to time. His handling of both the contract with Rague and the capitol construction funds had been criticized. Nevertheless, the majority report of an 1841 investigating committee exonerated Swan of all charges, and he remained in office until William B. Snyder was appointed building superintendent by the new territorial governor, John Chambers.

In 1842, Snyder located a second limestone quarry about ten miles northwest of Iowa City and determined that its stone was superior to that previously used (this despite the fact that both are identified geologically as the same member of the same period). This quarry, known today as the Old State Quarry, is now covered by the waters of the Coralville Reservoir. At that time, the stone was floated down the Iowa River on barges and then hauled up the bluff by oxen to the capitol site where it was cut. In 1842, thirty-two quarry labourers and fifty-seven boathands were on the capitol payroll, but—surprisingly—not one individual identified as a stonecutter was listed.

Under Snyder's supervision work progressed, and the roof of Allegheny pine shingles was placed on the capitol in September 1842. In his report to the legislature dated December 1, 1842, Snyder stated that the new capitol would be ready for the convening of the Fifth Legislative Assembly of the Territory of Iowa on December 5 of that year, although the building would be far from complete. The legislature had already moved from Burlington to Iowa City in time for the opening of the fourth legislative assembly, and its members were housed in temporary quarters, a frame hotel and tavern prepared for their use by one Walter Butler, to serve until the statehouse was completed. Four rooms on the first floor of the new building would be ready for use by the House of Representatives, the Council, the secretary of the territory, and the library. Still unfinished, however, were the west wall from the lower part of the second-floor windows, the projecting cornices, and the cupola, which was "completed to its first contraction or diminish, and temporarily covered."[15]

A report by Snyder dated January 16, 1843, furnished a detailed estimate for funds to complete the capitol. A total of $39,143 was needed to pay for forty-six windows with inside shutters on the first and second floors "according to the original plan," "2 galleries" on the second floor, stairs "from the first main floor to the balustrade on Cupalo" [*sic*], the north-end gable, the cornices on the building and porticos, the porticos, and the cupola.[16] Snyder's report carried an interesting statement:

> I have not been able to make an accurate estimate for the cupalo [*sic*], on account of there being no plan for the cupalo

(nor for anything else) in the Superintendent's office when I received it, and having enough to attend to through the season, I did not draw one. This report will not permit of delay, to give me sufficient time to draw a plan. But I presume the cupalo will not vary much from $4,000.00.[17]

His comments raise several questions. If he had received no plan for the cupola or "for anything else," how could he state that the windows with inside shutters would be made "according to the original plan"? Did Snyder himself design the cupola that was constructed? If he did not, who did?

William Snyder supervised the capitol construction for about a year and was then replaced by John M. Colman, the territorial agent. In 1843 Colman reported to the legislature that the north-end gable and chimneys were finished and that two additional rooms, not specified, were also completed, raising the number of usable rooms to six. He expressed concern about the foundation of the porticos on which the columns and pediments would eventually rest:

> These porticos were not constructed of the best materials, and especially the one on the west front, which is now so far injured as to render it necessary to rebuild it. The east front portico having been constructed of better materials, is not materially injured, and may be saved from loss by adding the steps and flagging to it the ensuing season.[18]

Eighty years later in the 1920s, almost identical comments would be made by the University's superintendent of buildings, who was then in charge of an extensive rehabilitation of Old Capitol. Perhaps because the porticos were primarily esthetic rather than functional, they were the last parts of the building to be finished according to Rague's plan. Clearly, funding continued to be a problem and depended to a great extent on the sale of Iowa City lots. In fact, many who contracted for the lots worked out the purchase price by hours of labor on the capitol. Their lack of training may explain why the construction of the porticos left something to be desired.

Colman and his successor as territorial agent, Anson Hart, re-

ported little accomplished on the construction of the capitol between 1843 and 1845. Both men cited lack of funds, both from the
federal government and the sale of lots, as the reason. Morgan
Reno, treasurer of the territory, expressed concern for the protec-
tion of the building in late 1845, and a year later he submitted the
following statement to Governor James Clarke:

> Nothing has been done on the Capitol this season for want of
> proper materials and funds to procure workmen. The building
> is in very unprotected condition, subject to the injury by
> storms, &c. It is to be hoped that the Legislature may make
> some provision for its completion; at least to complete it suffi-
> ciently to protect it from the weather.[19]

Funding was the core of the problem, to be sure, but the goal of
achieving statehood occupied much of the time and thoughts of the
territorial legislators and citizens during the mid-1840s. Two constitutional conventions were held in the capitol before a state
constitution was adopted, and the necessary articles were finally
approved for admission to the Union on December 28, 1846. On
that date the still incomplete capitol ceased being the "Third Territorial Capitol of Iowa" and became the "First State Capitol
of Iowa."

The general assembly of the new state appropriated funds total-
ing $5,000 in 1847 and 1848 for the completion of the building and
asked Morgan Reno to superintend the process. "In plain and sub-
stantial manner," Reno was directed to finish both the House and
Senate halls on the second floor and to procure desks and chairs to
furnish the two rooms and four committee rooms in the basement.
In 1849 an additional $3,000 was granted to complete the cupola,
the rooms for state officers, the Supreme Court chamber, and the
library, all on the first floor. Instructions to Joseph T. Fales, newly
appointed to the reinstituted position of superintendent of buildings, once more referred to completing the four committee rooms
in the basement and also to finishing "the halls leading to the several rooms, with the stairway to the second floor, according to the
original plan of the Building."[20] Here was another reference to the
original plan.

In 1851 William Pattee was named building superintendent, and $2,500 was appropriated to further his work. He was instructed to build "according to the original plan, the stairs necessary for said building; have finished the central hall leading to the cupola; and to have the public square [Capitol Square on the original plat] enclosed."[21] The original plan apparently still existed, if not on paper at least in someone's mind. In addition, the first concern for landscaping was stated.

A year later, the state legislature stipulated that $5,000 be expended under Pattee's guidance as follows:

> . . . in a permanent and workman-like manner, a gallery across the hall of the house of representatives, from east to west, and the necessary stairs leading thereto upon such plans as may be deemed most suitable; to have the porch upon the east and west sides of the capitol completed with stone steps, flagging, end walls, &c., according to the original design, except the columns and other work extending above the first floor; to have that part of the building above the second well-hole completed in a plain and substantial manner; and to have done such other work as may be necessary to complete and preserve said building.[22]

Clearly, the instructions to Pattee directed construction of the gallery in the House chamber, but no later references discuss the procedure or completion of a gallery. An 1853 daguerreotype shows that the east front porch had been erected (fig. 6). If the reference to "that part of the building above the second well-hole" means the cupola, then that too was completed as instructed, for the cupola visible today may be seen in the 1853 picture.

For an 1854 map entitled "Iowa City and Its Environs," George H. Yewell, a local artist, made drawings of outstanding Iowa City structures and placed them as a border around the existing town plat (fig. 7). A drawing of the state capitol was included, and the east front appears as it does today. The picture shows a completed portico with four fluted Doric columns beneath a projecting triangular pediment. It seems that between the dates of the 1853 daguerreotype and the 1854 map, the east portico must have been

6. *Isaac Wetherby daguerreotype of Old Capitol*
from the southeast, 1853.
Courtesy University of Iowa Archives.

added, despite the lack of written evidence directing this to be done. The detailed accuracy of Yewell's drawing could scarcely have been accomplished without his viewing the finished building or Rague's original plan.

The completion of Old Capitol may owe more to the efforts of William Pattee than has previously been credited. It appears that under his superintendency the east portico was completed and much of the original interior work done according to the plan.

Pattee was succeeded in 1855 by M. L. Morris, who served as state treasurer. An appropriation of $4,000 was made to repair the leaking roof and to finish the frequently mentioned area above the second well-hole. No other moneys were designated for completing the structure until 1858 when $3,000 was appropriated. By that time the long-proposed removal of the capital of Iowa to the Des Moines area had occurred.

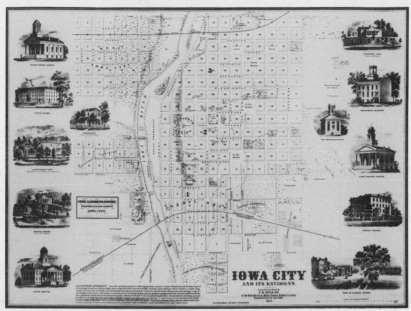

7. *J. H. Millar map, "Iowa City and Its Environs," 1854.*
Courtesy State Historical Society of Iowa, Iowa City.

Much of the material for the construction of Old Capitol was supplied by early Iowa City merchants, although records show that some materials were brought overland from Bloomington (Muscatine) by oxcart and stagecoach. Sylvanus Johnson, Iowa City's first brickmaker, fired about 60,000 soft bricks that were used for the interior walls of the building, according to expense accounts at the National Archives. Twenty thousand feet of oak flooring were purchased from John Ronalds, one of the original commissioners, and Hanby and Heron provided joists for the second floor. Other wood came from the mill of Henry Felkner.

Craftsmen who left an imprint on the appearance of Old Capitol included Michael Sydell, the contractor for the four large Doric columns of the east portico, and M. A. Foster, the carpenter who worked with him. The columns were made of a cypress core wrapped in a circular fluting of pine, as shown in the renovation

8. Construction of west portico columns, 1922.
Old Capitol Reconstruction Album.

photograph (fig. 8). Then paint was applied and sand blown onto the wet surface to give the appearance of stone.[23] The Corinthian columns surrounding the lantern portions of the cupola were carved from pine by Thomas M. Banbury, a carpenter. Anson Hart, an Iowa City tinner, placed the original metal, probably tin, on the roof of the cupola.[24] Three other craftsmen, William Windrem and Henry and R. R. Tillotson, worked on the spiral staircase.

Furnishings

The first furnishings for the new capitol in Iowa City were "left overs." The furniture and accessories had been used in the two Burlington churches that had housed the legislative bodies and in the rented rooms that had provided office space for officials, including the governor. They had also been used in Butler's hotel-and-tavern capitol, after being transferred to Iowa City by wagon.

Some items of furniture are listed on a bill of sale, dated April

15, 1839, from a St. Louis company, Lynch and Trask. Other pieces were handcrafted by a Burlington cabinetmaker, Evan Evans. Records show that he made "one table with drawers, one large writing desk, a case with pigeonholes and drawers, and one book-case" for Governor Lucas.[25] In addition, territorial expense accounts indicate payment to Evans "for making desks &c. for Legislature" and another payment "for Desks, bookcases &c." Based upon expense accounts, additional items brought from Burlington included maps, Franklin stoves, fireplace equipment, sperm candles, brass candlesticks, spittoons, and writing paper and equipment such as quill pens, black ink, and black sand.

Several early Iowa City cabinetmakers produced furniture for the new capitol in 1841. Thomas Snyder was paid $13 for making a writing desk, W. H. Patton made a table for the office of the secretary of the territory, and C. Ruggles received "$1.25 for making one desk stool." Jacob Boblitz made desks for the two chambers and for clerks and secretaries in 1850, and Charles Gaymon provided "twelve setts [sic] of chairs" in 1852. In 1855, Peter Roberts made a governor's desk and table as well as other desks for the capitol.

Carpeting had been purchased in 1839 for use in Burlington, 156 yards for the House chamber and 84 yards for the Council chamber. The kinds of carpeting were not indicated. In addition, 43 yards of Venetian carpeting were purchased that year, perhaps for the governor's office. Vouchers from the 1850s, marked both "purchased" and "made," suggest that commercially manufactured and homemade carpets, such as rag rugs, were used. Fabric for curtains and draperies of "velvet, sattinett, calico, marenoe, and chintz" had also been purchased, and Mrs. A. F. Hampton, Mrs. A. C. Allds, and Mrs. Holt were paid "for making curtains" and covers for desks.

Four fireplaces, one in each corner room of the first floor housing the secretary of state's office, the governor's office, the library, and the Supreme Court chamber, provided heat for Old Capitol. Wood-burning stoves were also installed elsewhere in the building. Candles and other lighting devices of the 1840 to 1850 period, such as whale-oil and Astral and Sinumbra lamps, provided light. One old settler also described a "chandelier" made of wood laths with nails driven through the laths from the underside to hold candles in place.

In November and December of 1857, the entire contents of the state property in the first capitol were loaded onto wagons and bobsleds for the westward move to Des Moines.

Historic Events

As soon as the capitol building was under construction, it immediately became the center of community life for the residents of Iowa City. By July 4, 1840, the foundation had been completed to the cornerstone level. In that year, the Fourth of July celebration commemorated the laying of the building's cornerstone, and an elaborate ceremony with many speeches was followed by a picnic on the grounds. This became an annual event for many years.

As soon as rooms were ready for occupancy in 1842, local churches of various denominations were given permission to hold worship services in the building. The House and Senate chambers were also used, once they were finished. This practice replaced holding religious services in homes, and it continued until church buildings were constructed in the town.

Old Capitol was also Iowa City's social center. In 1844 several sewing societies held a soiree and collation there that included "a fair for the sale of fancy and manufactured articles." In January 1847, the United States senator A. C. Dodge gave a ball to celebrate his re-election to the Senate by the Iowa legislature. The affair, attended by a large number of ladies and gentlemen, was described as follows:

> The desks were taken out of the Senate Chamber, and there was at the state house one of the largest and most beautiful parties that had ever been witnessed at the capital.[26]

Another ball celebrated the anniversary of George Washington's birthday in the House chamber "with a fine supper in the Senate

Chamber prepared by Charley Swan." On December 22, 1854, the citizens of Iowa City gave "a Social and Complimentary Party" in the statehouse to recognize the members of the legislature and other state officials. The Senate chamber was used for dancing, the House chamber was assigned for those who did not wish to dance, and supper was served in the basement.

In 1844 the town of Iowa City was allowed to occupy a basement room to house the Iowa City Fire Company No. 1 and to use the Supreme Court chamber for meetings of the Vigilance Committee of the Iowa City precinct. When the new state was just sixteen days old on January 18, 1847, the Anti-Capital Punishment and Prison Discipline Society held its annual meeting in Old Capitol with the chief justice of the Iowa Supreme Court, Charles Mason, as the featured speaker. He spoke in favor of abolishing capital punishment.

Many other historic events took place in the capitol during the territorial and statehood years, including the inauguration of all Iowa's governors—James Clarke in 1845, Ansel Briggs in 1846, Stephen Hempstead in 1850, and James W. Grimes in 1854. The building also housed three constitutional conventions held in 1844, 1846, and 1857. February 25, 1847, saw the founding of the State University of Iowa, and in 1848 the medical convention that organized a state medical society was held. The Iowa State Teachers Association was founded at Old Capitol in 1854, as were the Iowa Republican Party in 1856 and the State Historical Society of Iowa in 1857. Another important event was the celebration held in 1856 when the first train arrived in Iowa City!

Old Capitol had been given to the newly formed State University of Iowa in 1847 in the act that established the school. The same act, however, had specified that the state government would occupy the building "until otherwise provided for by law."[27] It thus continued as the "First State Capitol of Iowa" until December 1857, when the official seat of government moved to Des Moines. Only then, after serving for fifteen years as a capitol, did Old Capitol become the first permanent home of the young University of Iowa.

2. The University Years, 1857–1970

The capitol building was still unfinished when the State University of Iowa inherited it in December of 1857, but it was to be much more spacious than the rented quarters in Mechanics Academy had been. Although the University had existed on paper since its founding in 1847, it had held few classes and had graduated no students. At last, with a permanent structure as its home, the state's goals for providing college education in Iowa could be realized.

Two problems lay before the appointed board of trustees: to adapt the building, designed for governmental purposes, to educational use and to generate a student body. Because there were few high schools in Iowa at that time, there were few prospective University students. Thus, one of the first decisions of the trustees was to create a Normal Department for training teachers and a Preparatory Department or Model School where the teachers-in-training could practice. At the same time, of course, they would be developing students to enter college-level education. The Department of Ancient and Modern Languages and the Department of Mathematics and Natural Philosophy were also established.

The southeast room on the first floor of Old Capitol, which had formerly provided office space for the secretary of state, was remodeled to house the Normal Department. The remaining first-floor rooms were used as recitation rooms by the other departments.

On the second floor, the House chamber at the south end was converted into a chapel where mandatory chapel exercises were held daily. The companion room at the north end of the floor, the Senate chamber, was divided into two rooms with the University library assigned to the west side and the "Natural History Cabinet" to the east.[1] The University's prized collection of geological specimens was housed there. An early Iowa City contracting firm, Finkbine and Lovelace, was in charge of the remodeling.

Old Capitol was thus the physical entirety of the University of Iowa in the 1857–1858 academic year, when it opened its doors to 107 students, 59 gentlemen and 48 ladies.

Early Room Usage

No room was assigned to the first president of the University, Amos Dean, since he was not a president in residence. Although he had accepted the responsibilities of the office when appointed in 1855, Dean believed that he could combine them with his position as chancellor of the Albany Law School in New York. University records show that Dean visited the Iowa campus three times before resigning in 1859. Although he did not have or need an office, Dean apparently had a walnut armchair with a caned seat. It was preserved in Old Capitol throughout the years and today is in the president's office in the southeast corner of the first floor.

Within just one year, despite the few academic offerings, the University was ready to graduate its first student. Dexter Edson Smith, the only graduate, received the Bachelor of Science degree on July 7, 1858, during ceremonies held in the House chamber.

Shortly thereafter, following Amos Dean's advice, the board of trustees agreed that the University should close its doors temporarily. Time was needed for building a solid financial base and for students enrolled in the Normal Department to become qualified for a University education. The University did not reopen until the fall of 1860.

In the meantime, the capitol building provided space for the State Historical Society of Iowa. Its first quarters were in a ground-floor room in the southwest corner. A year later the society was moved to the second floor, where it shared the room occupied by the University library. This arrangement proved inadequate, and the board of the society petitioned in 1859 for use of an empty recitation room. This was granted, and the society moved into the large northeast-corner room, the former Supreme Court chamber. When the University reopened following its two-year closure, it had vastly improved its financial structure and had enlarged its student body. All recitation rooms were thus required, including the Supreme Court chamber, and the society moved off campus to quarters in the Mechanics Academy in 1862.

The Normal Department and the Model School had continued to operate during the time the University was closed, in accordance with Dean's concern for an adequately prepared student body. The Normal Department moved to the room occupied by the University library, the west half of the old Senate chamber. That room was furnished with thirty double desks and seats, which were described locally as "of Eastern manufacture, in a style of neatness and convenience equal perhaps to any in the State or of the West."[2]

The Model School was located in the southeast quadrant of the basement in 1859, directly beneath the first site of the Normal Department. It remained there until 1863 when it was moved to the Mechanics Academy to share that building with the State Historical Society.

During the two years that the University was closed, the board of trustees undertook numerous improvements in Old Capitol. In 1859 they indicated in their meeting minutes a concern for esthetics, "for youth are educated through the eye as well as the mind." A new staircase to the basement was built, and in the recitation rooms the walls were painted and the ceilings whitewashed. The paint colors selected are not known, since official records refer only to "colored" walls. One room, the chapel, received a frescoed treatment at the hands of a Mr. Munro, who was supervised by board member Hugh D. Downey, an influential Iowa City lawyer and banker.

One University alumnus, reminiscing about his experiences as a student in the Normal Department in 1858, wrote that "at this time a number of students lived and boarded themselves in vacant rooms of Capitol Building." This is the first—and perhaps the only—indication that Old Capitol had provided housing for students.

Silas Totten, an Episcopal priest, was serving as the second president of the University when it reopened in the fall of 1860. He was an on-the-scene president and required an office. Totten selected the corner portion of the large southeast room on the first floor, and it was partitioned off from the rest of the room. This was to become a historic part of Old Capitol, for all presidents of the University prior to the 1970s' restoration used the room as an office. One can only speculate about the many decisions, made in that small room, that determined the course of the University.

Expansion of the University's instructional departments accompanied the reopening, and specific rooms were assigned to professors to serve as both offices and classrooms. On the first floor, Professor D. Franklin Wells, who had served as principal of the Normal Department beginning in 1856, occupied the room north of the president's office. Across the hall to the west, the Reverend Oliver M. Spencer taught Greek and modern languages in the old governor's office, while next door the auditor's office provided a classroom for political economy, taught by President Totten. On the north side of the lobby, Spencer taught Latin in the former treasurer's office, and N. R. Leonard offered mathematics in the former territorial–state library. The Supreme Court chamber served as a history classroom and housed the State Historical Society. It was also a meeting site for the University's early literary societies—the Zetagathian, Erodelphian, and Hesperian societies and the Irving Institute.

The University's curator and librarian, Theodore S. Parvin, was in charge of natural history courses and was assigned to the Natural History Cabinet on the second floor. In 1838 Parvin had assembled the first library for the Iowa Territory at the request of Governor Lucas. When he achieved professorial status, he moved to the Supreme Court chamber, and this was the only major change in the use of first- and second-floor rooms in the early 1860s.

Beginning in 1859, the north end of the ground floor provided a residence for the University's janitor, his family, and a dog. The

University purchased the dog for $5 in order to "keep horses, cattle, and other livestock off the grounds." One of the janitors apparently was a Mr. Roupee, for an 1867 notice in the *Iowa City Republican* read: "The ladies of the Congregational Church will hold a sociable at the rooms of Mrs. Roupee, in the U. building, [Old Capitol] entrance at north end, this Wed. evening. They invite all their friends to attend."[3]

The first record of a bell purchased and presumably hung in the cupola of Old Capitol dates from April 1861, when a bell weighing 1,100 pounds was obtained for $360. Its ringing to signal the opening and closing of classes became one of the University's fondest traditions and still endures today. In the 1860s the custodian climbed to the cupola to ring the bell by hand, but today it is rung electronically. A second bell was purchased in 1864 and a third, the one still in use, in 1901.

Campus Expansion

The opening in 1863 of South Hall, a four-story brick building directly south of Old Capitol, brought about major changes in Old Capitol's role as the "total" University, or nearly so. South Hall was constructed to be a boarding house primarily, but it was not long before several recitation rooms were transferred there, among them rooms for three lady teachers in the Normal and Preparatory Departments and for the male teacher of vocal and instrumental music. The literary societies were also assigned space on the fourth floor. In fact, the University was growing not only in the diversity of course offerings but in the number of students enrolled. There were 668 resident students by 1866, and duplicate chapel services were scheduled in South Hall since the University chapel (formerly the House chamber) could not accommodate everyone at one sitting.

A second brick building, named North Hall, was first occupied in 1866 (fig. 9). It stood directly north of Old Capitol. Initially the new building provided space for a chapel, classrooms for chemistry

*9. University of Iowa campus, c. 1870: South Hall,
Central Hall (Old Capitol), and North Hall.*
Old Capitol Reconstruction Album.

and "philosophical apparatus," and a basement storeroom for geological specimens before their removal to the Natural History Cabinet. Again, Old Capitol's role changed, with much of the vacated space becoming new recitation rooms. The Cabinet of Geology and Mineraloy [*sic*] was assigned to the former chapel, and geology professor Charles A. White was given the room occupied by the cabinet. This arrangement did not last long, however, because of the addition of new University departments.

The report of an 1866 legislative committee whose members visited the University campus recommended several improvements for the main building, Old Capitol. One was the installation of a furnace to replace the many wood- and coal-burning cast-iron stoves throughout the structure. At some time the four fireplaces on the first floor had been bricked in, but it is not known when this occurred. The pine-shingled roof had sprung leaks that were damaging the "elegant fresco work" in some of the classrooms, and it was replaced with a new slate roof. The furnace cost $2,000 and the new roof $3,000.

A third recommendation called for the erection of a new building at the rear of Old Capitol for use as "a wood-house, coal-bin, &c., and as the present water-closets are wholly insufficient, being exposed to view, and altogether too small, the proposed building might be so arranged as to provide suitable accommodations for both sexes separate from each other."[4] This was one of the small ancillary buildings that are visible on the west side of Old Capitol in some late nineteenth century photographs.

An Iowa Law School had been established in Des Moines in 1866 by two justices of the Iowa Supreme Court, and they petitioned the state legislature for permission to affiliate the school with the University in Iowa City. Two years later, the legislature approved an appropriation of $20,000 to enable the school to merge with the University that year. The new Law Department was assigned to Old Capitol's House chamber, which was divided into three rooms. The largest room, on the west side and about two-thirds the size of the original chamber, was designated a lecture and recitation room. Desks for forty to fifty students were installed there with considerable room available for a larger student body. The eastern third of the room was divided in two, with one room serving as an office for the three faculty members and the other as the law library.[5]

Eventually University authorities focused their attention on landscaping and improving the area surrounding the University buildings. Few sidewalks had existed previously, but it was necessary to connect the three structures. So-called concrete sidewalks made of a combination of sand and coal tar were installed first. These did not last well, however, and in 1876 they were replaced by limestone slabs obtained from a Joliet, Illinois, quarry. The slabs were eight feet long, five to eight feet wide, and about five inches thick. Most of these slab sidewalks served the University well, and the last one—the sidewalk extending from Old Capitol east to Clinton Street—was not removed until 1975.

10. East facade of Old Capitol before 1900.
T. W. Townsend stereopticon slide.
Courtesy State Historical Society of Iowa, Iowa City.

An iron fence surrounded the campus in the 1860s, and people had to climb over stiles, set at intervals around the four-block area. In 1872 the general assembly provided funding for another iron fence, and the following year "a double wire fence" was also installed around the periphery of the campus to protect new trees that were being planted in the parking area (fig. 10).

Two gas lamps were installed in 1877, one north and one south of University Hall, as Old Capitol had come to be called. These supplemented the first outdoor gas lights that had been placed at the

Clinton Street and Iowa Avenue entrance to the campus by the city gas company in 1874.

Despite the addition of the two new buildings in the 1860s, the space did not keep pace with the growth of the University and the needs of its programs, old and new. The Law Department was in dire need of more space and was granted use of the recitation room north of the president's office in 1876 for the second-year advanced law class. Later the department was permitted to partition off a part of the west side of the second-floor lobby for a small classroom. At the same time, the west side of the first-floor hall became a room used as an armory.

The University library, too, was bursting at the proverbial seams. In 1878, 8,500 books were housed in the room in the old Senate chamber that was just forty-two feet by twenty-seven feet. The board of regents approved "fitting up" the north end of the first floor of the capitol, creating a library on the west side of the hall and a reading room on the east.

Major changes in the early 1880s saw the University library move again from the north end on the first floor of Old Capitol to the second-floor chapel room of North Hall. That room was divided in two, the north half housing the library stacks and the south half becoming a combined reading room and chapel. The first-floor rooms left vacant in Old Capitol were turned over to geology professor Samuel Calvin and made into a "lecture room, laboratory, working cabinet, and working library" for the Department of Natural Science. The Natural History Cabinet remained directly above on the second floor, and the room west of it was assigned to the Law Department, which moved its library there. In 1886 the new Science Hall on the northeast quadrant of the campus was opened, and both the Natural History Cabinet and the Natural Science Department were moved there. The former cabinet room became a lecture room for advanced law, and the first-floor rooms vacated by the Natural Science Department became recitation rooms.

One Old Capitol room, the first-floor room to the left of the east entrance and adjacent to the president's office, served a surprising use—that of a gymnasium! This is recorded in two different sources, the minutes of the board of trustees and the memoirs of a former University student as reported in the *Iowa Alumnus*. The two references, one in 1866 and the other in 1888, indicated that gymnastics equipment was installed there and could be used "on permission." But most frequently the space was described as a recitation or law classroom until 1900.

Over the years, the administration of the University grew in numbers as did the faculty and the student body. There was a need for more offices, and beginning in the late 1890s, the secretary of the University, William J. Haddock, was assigned to the northeast room of the first floor, the former Supreme Court chamber. To house additional administrative officials, rooms continued to be divided and halls partitioned. The president remained in his traditional quarters, and the University secretary stayed in the corresponding northeast area. On the first floor, the superintendent of buildings and grounds and the janitor occupied two rooms in the northwest quadrant. There was also a small security room that housed a vault, as well as another room labeled "Private," on the floor plan, presumably a restroom. The north–south hall was partitioned into a supply room and a second private room.

In the southwest quadrant, the board room remained where the governor's office had been originally, but the adjacent auditor's office had been turned over to the dean of the College of Liberal Arts. In addition, the dean had a private office in adjoining space cut off from the main lobby and created when walls were installed across the hall between the Doric columns. A second office, used by the University's finance committee, was made by closing the west entrance and erecting a dividing wall there.

The two large chambers remained on the second floor, the south one designated for assemblies and the north one as the registrar's office. The second-floor lobby was partitioned at each end to create two small rooms. The two at the east end were occupied by the secretary of the Alumni Bureau of Information and his staff. One of the rooms at the west end was used by Professor Forrest Ensign. The second one housed the stairs to the cupola and was so small that it would have been quite undesirable. There is no information about how it was actually used.

At the turn of the century, the University campus consisted of six academic buildings in the four-block area. Five of them were in a straight line north and south facing Clinton Street. The Dental Building was the farthest north, followed by North Hall, Central Hall (Old Capitol renamed), South Hall, and the Medical Building. Science Hall, situated as it was between the Dental Building and Clinton Street, must have appeared poorly located and out-of-place (fig. 11). Close to and west of Old Capitol were a heating plant and several maintenance buildings. Southwest and between it and South Hall was an impressive structure—the University Water Closet, or restroom. The plans of this much-needed building exist today, while those of Old Capitol do not! Frequent references to the structure have been found, including one which nicknamed the building "the twenty-four holer" (fig. 12).

In 1901 a disastrous fire struck the campus, destroying both the Medical Building and South Hall. Another fire had occurred four years previously in North Hall, and though that building was not destroyed, many of the library's books were either destroyed or water-soaked. One University official recalled that the basement floors of Old Capitol were covered with open books, and that even though it was July, the furnace was turned on to hasten the drying-out process.

By that time, the board of trustees had already worked for many years to create a plan for the development of the central campus and had involved the noted architect, Henry Van Brunt, in advising them. Apparently, he suggested the five-building composition for the central campus, with a new building at each of Old Capitol's four corners. The first to be completed was located southeast of Old Capitol and closer to Clinton Street. It was to be named the Hall of Liberal Arts or the Collegiate Building, and it later became Schaeffer Hall. When it was completed in 1902, all remaining academic departments in Old Capitol except the Law Department were moved there.

Thus, only the newly named College of Law and the University administration occupied Old Capitol. In 1903, the partition separating the library and the advanced law lecture room was removed, and the entire former Senate chamber was remodeled as

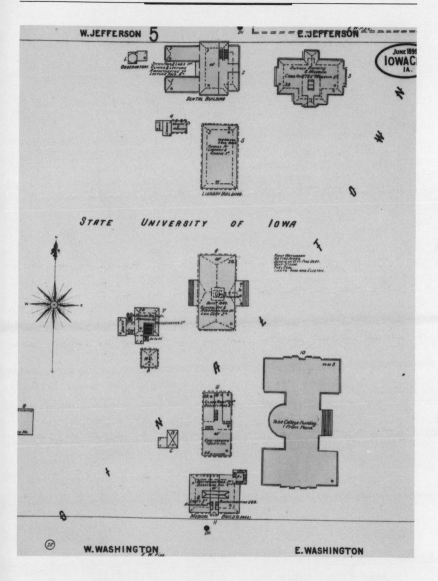

11. *Sanborn fire map of the Pentacrest, 1899. Major buildings from north to south are: top left, Old Dental Building; top right, Science Hall (Calvin Hall); North Hall (Library Building); Central Hall (Old Capitol); South Hall; Medical Building. At bottom right is the proposed Collegiate Building (Schaeffer Hall).*
Courtesy State Historical Society of Iowa, Iowa City.
Photo Craig Kohl, University Photo Service.

12. East facade, showing University Water Closet at far left, n.d.
Courtesy University of Iowa Archives.

the law library. The College of Law remained in the building until 1910, when it moved to the newly constructed Law Building at the northeast corner of the Capitol and Jefferson streets intersection.

The second of the four new buildings constructed around Old Capitol, the Natural Science Building (now Macbride Hall) was completed and occupied in 1906. Its location, which was planned to balance the Collegiate Building, had made it necessary to either tear down or move the 1886 Science Hall. The latter course was chosen, and the building—with its complete contents remaining inside—was moved to the northwest corner of the Capitol and Jefferson streets intersection in 1905. A mastermind must have engineered the move, for it was reported that not a single test tube or beaker was broken and no chemicals spilled as the building was rolled to its new location. Eventually, the building housed the Geology Department and was named in honor of Samuel Calvin. Today the University's admissions offices are located there. The final two buildings in the plan for the Pentacrest, MacLean Hall and Jessup Hall, were completed in 1912 and 1924 respectively.

Incidentally, the name *Pentacrest* resulted from a competition sponsored by the *Daily Iowan* to find a more dignified name for the area, which was popularly referred to as "Five Spot." Benjamin F. Shambaugh believed that the only appropriate title was Old Capitol Campus. Other suggestions included the Pentagon, the Mall, the Bowl, and the Oval (in reference to the area directly south of Old Capitol, which was used for dramatic presentations and May fetes). But a student developed the word *Pentacrest*, and it has been known by that name ever since.[6]

The University's commitment to planning the campus also extended to landscaping. Early in the twentieth century, the nationally known landscape firm, the Olmsted Brothers of New York, was invited to develop landscaping ideas. They presented their proposal in 1905, recommending that Old Capitol always be the central focus of the campus. They also suggested that land be acquired on the west side of the Iowa River and that a building with a tower be built there to complement Old Capitol.

Various steps toward modernizing campus buildings were also taken in the late nineteenth and early twentieth centuries. In 1889 the regents authorized the first telephone on campus for the president's office, and additional telephones were added in Old Capitol in 1905. Restroom facilities were initially placed in the building in 1904 when the regents had two water closets installed at unidentified locations. These supplemented the one-story brick building directly south of Old Capitol that served the entire campus. The first reference to electricity occurred in 1905, when the board of regents "discussed possibilities of electric lights for Old Capitol." They were installed in the law library and in the office of the dean of the College of Law in 1906, but no reference to their being placed in the president's office has been found.

Furnishings

Only a few interior photographs of Old Capitol have been located to provide primary source information about its furnishings during University days in the nineteenth and early twentieth centuries.

13. Junior law classroom (House chamber), c. 1889.
Courtesy University of Iowa Law Library.

The earliest interior view found so far shows the House chamber as used by junior law students in 1889 (fig. 13). The Windsor arm-chairs, often referred to today as firehouse Windsors, each had an attached writing surface. The instructor presided on a raised platform at a small slant-topped desk placed parallel to the south wall in front of a series of blackboards. Some blackboards were fastened to the wall and some were placed in three window openings in front of the inside louvered shutters. The latter had at some time replaced the original solid-panel shutters. Gas lighting fixtures hung from the ceiling, and the floors were uncarpeted. A few decorative objects were used, including photographs taken annually of members of the law graduating classes.

Another picture of a classroom taken about 1900 shows the only evidence of the use of frescoes in Old Capitol (fig. 14). Here they appear as a border. According to a secondary source, this room

*14. Political science classroom of Benjamin F. Shambaugh, c. 1900.
Location unsure but probably in northwest quadrant of first floor.
Courtesy University of Iowa Archives.*

served at the time as a political science classroom for Professor
Benjamin F. Shambaugh.

A picture of the executive committee of the board of regents,
taken about 1894 in the board room (located where the governor's
office had been in the southwest corner of the first floor), shows two
chairs with caned or wicker backs and a large conference table, as
well as the original solid-panel window shutters (fig. 15). The chair
at the right is identical in all details to one that Willard and Susan
Boyd later located and gave to Old Capitol for use in the president's office. A chair visible in the center of the picture was high-
backed and featured incised details typical of the time. The conference table is still in use in Old Capitol in the administrative
offices on the ground floor, although for some years it was used by
the College of Law. It was about to be disposed of in the mid-1970s
when Boyd spotted it and returned it to Old Capitol. This picture

15. Board of regents meeting in Old Capitol board room
(governor's office), c. 1894. Left to right: Wm. J. Haddock,
board secretary; Colonel Albert W. Swalm; D. N. Richardson;
and Howard A. Burrell. An original picture hangs in the
Old Capitol administrative office.

of the board room, incidentally, provides the only evidence that
wallpaper was used in Old Capitol. Visible on the rear wall, the
wallpaper was designed with a Renaissance Revival pattern popular in the late nineteenth century. The floor covering in the board
room was of a woven hemp material.

The law library was located in the north chamber on the second
floor, the former Senate chamber, from 1880 to 1910. A 1905 photograph from the University annual, *The Hawkeye*, shows dramatically how the room was adapted for library purposes (fig. 16). A
balcony encircled the entire room and crossed each window about
three feet below the top. Access to the balcony was from staircases
at the east and west ends of the room. Book stacks at the floor level
were between the windows on the east, north, and west walls and
across the east and west doors on the south wall, leaving the central doorway as the point of entry to the room. In 1905 the library

16. College of Law Library (Senate chamber), 1905.
Courtesy University of Iowa Archives.

contained approximately 10,000 volumes. The library furniture
consisted of large oak tables and numerous chairs of several types,
some high-backed, others of a modified Windsor style.

One important piece of Old Capitol furniture used today came
from the office of William J. Haddock, secretary to the board of
regents from 1864 to 1902. His office was one of three rooms partitioned from the former Supreme Court chamber. In it was a large
walnut desk with leather inlaid in the slanted top, bookshelves
above, and numerous drawers and cupboard areas beneath. This
desk was given to the University by Haddock's descendants and
has been placed in the museum's reception area adjacent to the
president's office. Also in the reception area is a walnut armchair
that was used in the Normal Department in the 1870s or 1880s.

Historic Events

Until South Hall was opened in 1863, Old Capitol was the entire
University. It thus provided space for classrooms, offices, chapel

services, and meetings of the faculty, the board of regents, and the student literary societies—all the various activities associated with the young University. It also was the focal point for many historic events.

In 1864 President Lincoln requested volunteers for 100 days of military service to support the Union cause. Forty-five University students responded, along with nearly as many from Western and Cornell Colleges. On the steps of Old Capitol, they became Company D of the Fourth Regiment of the Iowa Infantry. Many years later, a president of the University wrote vividly of the building's role during the War between the States in his plea to establish a war memorial on the campus:

> . . . nearly every able-bodied man left the campus and donned the uniform of blue. Then when tidings of victory came, from every window of Old Capitol gleamed the light of many candles set there by the hands of loyal women and girls whose task it was "to keep the home fires burning."[7]

Frequent references to the involvement of the building—inside and out—in wartime preparations and events also appeared in newspapers published during World War I and World War II as well as during the Korean War and Vietnam War.

During World War I, there was a nationwide search for scraps of wood from historic sites to bring attention to the Liberty Loan Drive. President Walter A. Jessup removed a piece of wood from Old Capitol and sent it to Washington, D.C., to be burned in a bonfire to further the cause. In fact, throughout the war, the building displayed a visible recognition of the University's involvement:

> During the last year [1918] and more, from the pillars has floated a great service flag, bearing constant testimony that our boys were remembered, the golden evidence too of those who will not come back.[8]

In World War II, a United States Navy Pre-Flight unit was commissioned at the University in 1942, and before it was closed in late 1945 more than 21,000 cadets were trained on campus. Just like generations of other students, many cadets found the west steps of Old Capitol a favorite place to relax and to court University women students.

In 1970 a rally protesting the United States involvement in the Vietnam War was held on the east side of Old Capitol. The protestors entered the building and damaged several portraits, but they did not succeed in closing the University.

More than a century earlier, the University had closed its doors to mark a historic event. April 17, 1865, was a day of national mourning for Abraham Lincoln, victim of an assassin's bullet. The University honored the slain president by canceling classes and conducting memorial services jointly with the city on the east portico of Old Capitol. The east facade of the building was draped with black swags inscribed with the words, "Hung Be the Heavens All in Black," and all faculty members wore black and white rosettes as symbols of mourning (fig. 17). History repeated itself on November 25, 1963, when the University held a memorial service in the identical spot for John F. Kennedy, another president killed by an assassin. The thousands who participated will long remember the University of Iowa band's muffled drums and slow-paced, measured tread (fig. 18).

Old Capitol has also been used to honor a number of important "births." In 1925 the School of Religion was founded there. At the time of Iowa City's centennial in 1939, a series of events commemorated the occasion with Old Capitol as the focal point. One was the production of a historical pageant, "The Old Stone Capitol Remembers," based upon Benjamin F. Shambaugh's book by the same name. The State Historical Society of Iowa has held meetings in the building to recognize the 100th and 125th anniversaries of its founding there. In 1959, the American College Testing Program was also founded within Old Capitol's walls.

Over the years, conferences of national importance have often been held in Old Capitol's large second-floor chambers. The first National Arts Conference was held in 1928, and sculptor Lorado Taft was the featured speaker. The Ninth Annual Conference of History and Social Studies occurred in 1929. Through the 1920s

17. *Memorial service for Abraham Lincoln, April 17, 1865.*
Courtesy University of Iowa Archives.

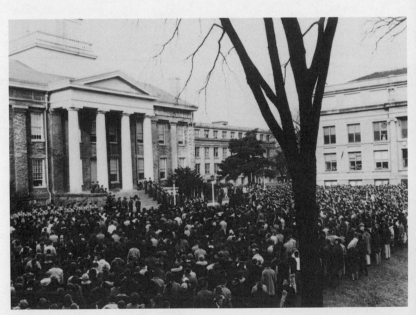

18. *Memorial service for John F. Kennedy, November 25, 1963.*
Courtesy University of Iowa Archives.

and 1930s, a series of Commonwealth Conferences and Round Table discussions were organized by Benjamin F. Shambaugh.

Many lecturers of national and international importance have also spoken in the building. Representative of the long list of notables are naturalist and geologist Louis Agassiz (1862 and 1864); Princess Julia Cantacuzene, granddaughter of Ulysses S. Grant and wife of a Russian prince, who spoke about Russia during the Bolshevik Revolution (1925); explorers Donald MacMillan (1926), Vilhjalmur Stefansson, and Roald Amundsen (1930); novelists Hugh Walpole (1927), Thornton Wilder (1927), and Emil Ludwig (1928); poets John Drinkwater (1925), and George W. Russell, known by his pseudonym "AE" (1930); and architect Frank Lloyd Wright (1939). Political figures who have campaigned from Old Capitol's east portico include Herbert Hoover (1928), Norman Thomas (1930), Nelson Rockefeller (1968), and George McGovern (1972).

Many other less historic but nonetheless important events took place at Old Capitol. University athletic contests were often held in its shadow. An Iowa City lawyer and graduate of the class of 1896, Samuel D. Whiting, reminisced about this in 1927:

> The athletic field was between Old Capitol and Madison Street. The baseball diamond was laid out on what is now the terrace to the central building.
>
> The distance between the pitcher's box and home plate was level, but one had to run up hill from second to third base and down hill from third to home place. . . .
>
> Tennis was introduced to the students of the university in a unique manner. The university offered to let any organization that would furnish its own net mark out a court on the east side of Old Capitol. I have seen as many as ten games in progress at once in the 'front yard' of Old Capitol.[9]

Innumerable pep meetings took place, and the traditional tug-of-war in the late 1880s between the law and medical students frequently was held in front of the east portico. Today, frisbee-throwing contests develop spontaneously on the nearby lawns.

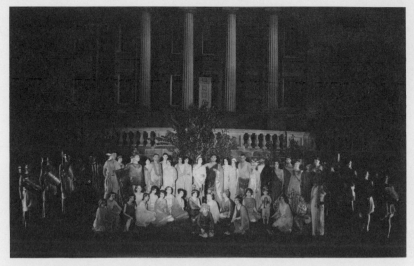

19. *Department of Speech and Dramatic Art, cast for Shakespeare's*
A Midsummer Night's Dream, *west terrace, 1930.*
Courtesy University of Iowa Archives.

In the late 1920s, a terrace was built adjacent to the west portico, and this area replaced the Old Capitol oval south of the building as the site for many outdoor University events, including dramatic productions. One was *A Midsummer Night's Dream,* staged in 1930 by the Department of Speech and Dramatic Art (fig. 19).

Old Capitol has also provided a background for numerous student pranks. In the late nineteenth century, these were considered so much a part of campus life that they were reported in the University newspaper and recorded in the memoirs of former students. The nearby cannon would be fired in the middle of the night. A straw dummy would be thrown from a cupola window and then replaced on the ground with a live, made-up "victim" before spectators arrived. And repeatedly, men students would "ogle" the ladies from the second-floor windows and the porticos.

In more recent years, Old Capitol has been the site of student demonstrations. Before the 1970 antiwar protest, students had poured blood on the east steps to protest the presence of marine recruiters on the campus in 1967. In 1969, a student had entered the building and attempted to arrest President Howard R. Bowen for not disclosing what the student considered to be public information. In recent years, students from foreign countries have gathered on Old Capitol's east side to mark major events in their home countries, and religious fanatics have appeared there regularly in support of their beliefs.

Despite occasional upheavals, the traditional events of the University have continued. And despite the building's various name changes—from the officially designated University Hall to the more generic University Building, Capitol Building, and Middle Building—Old Capitol has endured as the recognized center of University activity.[10] Graduations were held there until 1905, when the ceremony was moved to the first men's gymnasium, the Old Armory. Induction Day ceremonies have been held on the west or east portico at the beginning of the academic year, and the College of Law has sponsored an annual Supreme Court Day. Honorary societies have welcomed new members there, and doctoral students have defended their dissertations. Year after year, meetings have been held at Old Capitol by the Faculty Senate, the Student Senate, and the College of Liberal Arts faculty. Although many events have been held elsewhere to accommodate larger audiences as the University has grown, Old Capitol continues to be the focal point of the University of Iowa.

3. The Rehabilitation, 1921–1924

After the turn of the century, various newspapers, alumni publications, and board of trustees minutes recorded the need to preserve Old Capitol and to repair and fireproof the structure. There had been fires in several University buildings, and in 1914 a fire developed in a carpenter shop near Old Capitol. Despite fears that the building could not be saved, it survived, although the shop was completely razed.

Supporters took the cause to the Iowa legislature in 1915, and Senator O. A. Byington of Iowa City voiced the general concern. It was said that Old Capitol "has been struck by lightning and has had narrow escapes from destruction." One of them had occurred during a severe storm about 1910 when lightning did strike the building. Afterward, the Iowa Board of Education hired the Des Moines architectural firm, Proudfoot, Bird, and Rawson, to prepare exact drawings of Old Capitol, including all details, so that in the event of another similar disaster the building could be reproduced. This was foresighted indeed. A portion of those plans, dated 1912, exist today, and they provide helpful information about Old Capitol as it was in the early twentieth century.[1]

A four-page editorial in the February 1916 issue of the *Iowa Alumnus* pled eloquently for preservation and rehabilitation of the building:

> This state building, with all its historic associations, is in constant danger of destruction by fire. . . . Three quarters of

a century have so dried the flimsy upper weatherboarding and the massive timbers constituting the framework that the fire danger is much to be dreaded.

Look at the pictures accompanying this article. Do you wonder that a visitor who saw them while this article was being written should have asked in all seriousness, "Whose barn loft is that?" Think of these dry and exposed timbers covered with the dust and cobwebs of seventy-five years and then try to imagine the probable results of a lightning stroke or the effect of exposed wires. Already within the last decade, lightning has twice struck the old dome, and the miracle is that the building escaped destruction either time.[2]

Finally, on July 6, 1917, the legislators approved a $50,000 appropriation for "restoring, fireproofing, and remodeling" the former capitol. They acted largely because Iowans expressed their concerns and Byington persisted in pleading the case and in increasing the amount of the appropriation from the original asking. The involvement of the United States in World War I, however, delayed the beginning of preservation efforts until 1921.

Official documents referred to the renovation of Old Capitol in the 1920s as "repairs and fireproofing." Newspapers of the time, including the *Daily Iowan*, frequently reported on the "restoration" of the building. But it was not a restoration, since restoration is defined as "returning a structure to its appearance at a previous time."[3] A large part of the work authorized by the 1917 act of the Iowa general assembly was to adapt Old Capitol to the administrative needs of the University. At the time the administration included thirteen departments and a total of seventy-five employees.[4]

The legislators who drafted and approved the 1917 act were well aware of the historic and esthetic significance of Old Capitol, as section three of the act clearly indicates:

Limitation on reconstruction. That in the reconstruction of said building, the exterior shall not be changed in its appearance, structure or design and only such change shall be made in the interior of said building as is necessary to properly carry out the purpose and intent of this act to make said building fireproof or substantially so and to reproduce said structure without change in any of its original parts.[5]

Generations of Iowans are now and will be forever in their debt.

The renovation was carried out in a manner true to the direction the legislature had mandated. No changes in Old Capitol's exterior appearance, structure, or design were made, other than the addition of the always-intended west portico. However, in the building's interior, many alterations were made in room arrangement and detail "as [were] necessary to properly carry out the purpose and intent of this act." Presumably, the planning committee justified each change as needed for fireproofing or for replacing or reproducing worn-out and disintegrated materials. Other changes were introduced to provide adequate space to house the various departments.

The University's superintendent of buildings and grounds, A. A. Smith, supervised Old Capitol's renovation. A remark in his report on the project—"no definite plan or scheme [for the renovation] could be laid out in advance until the condition of the walls and timber construction were discovered as the work progressed"—showed both wisdom and foresight.[6] In fact, a second appropriation of $50,000 in 1923 would be necessary before the rehabilitation could be completed.

Structural Rehabilitation

One of the first major problems encountered was the settling the building had experienced since its construction in the 1840s. The original foundation extended only five feet below ground level, and the weight of the heavy limestone resting upon this shallow footing was so great that settling had occurred and large cracks had developed in the walls (fig. 20). Settling was also caused by the below-ground tunnels that carried electrical and plumbing conduits from one University building to another.

20. *House chamber showing large crack over window*
near southwest corner, 1921.
Old Capitol Reconstruction Album.

21. Southwest corner braced for raising, 1921.
Old Capitol Reconstruction Album.

22. Jack screws in place to raise southwest corner, 1921.
Old Capitol Reconstruction Album.

Examination revealed that Old Capitol's southwest corner was eight inches lower than its northeast corner and that the entire southwest quarter-section of the building had settled another three inches (fig. 21). In addition to the cracks in the masonry work, the floors and doors were out of line. The main spiral staircase, which had been repaired at some time in the building's eighty-one year history, was found to need one more step than it had had originally—twenty-six instead of twenty-five.

To solve the settling problem, the project crew decided to raise the entire quarter-section back into place and to build a completely new foundation to support it. The corner was braced by large wooden timbers, and steel beams were placed under the stone walls. Three hundred jacks for turning and raising the corner were positioned under the new supports, some on the inside of the wall and others on the outside (fig. 22). On a given signal, each worker turned a single jack a specified number of revolutions, and in time the deed was accomplished. The workers raised an estimated 6,300 tons by this process. They worked meticulously and even cleaned out the cracks in the walls before raising the corner, thus preventing foreign material from being caught in the

cracks and detracting from the esthetic appearance of the limestone walls. Coincidentally, Rague's Illinois capitol of 1837 also experienced extensive settling, and the problem was corrected in the
same way.

Old Capitol's other exterior problems involved the roof and
cupola areas. The original pine roof had been covered with a layer
of pine sheathing, over which had been laid a slate roof. The
weight on the trusses and purlins (the horizontal supports) beneath
had forced them out of true. Moreover, patching had been done
periodically, and additional roofs had been added. To make the
roof fireproof, all layers of roofing were first removed. Steel rods
were installed to reinforce the trusses supporting the roof rafters,
and a new slate roof was installed. The first slate roof bore the word
IOWA spelled in light-colored slate against a dark background, but
that legend had been destroyed by storms and breakage.[7]

The original main gutter around the building and the down-
spouts had been hewn out of walnut logs. Because of their rotted
condition, they were replaced with copper.

The cupola presented a serious structural problem, and rehabilitation workers wondered why the joints and supports in the
area had not given way. The architects decided to replace the old
wooden timbers with new steel posts that would rest upon a separate concrete foundation at the basement level. The vertical supports would be concealed in the north and south walls of the
central halls. The separate concrete foundation would support a
fireproof slab of concrete under the cupola area. Also, the architects predicted that future generations would wish to replace the
cupola's sixteen painted and sanded Corinthian columns, which
were made of pine, with duplicates of cut stone. It would then be
necessary to have such a foundation to support the added weight.
The technique of treating wood to look like stone was a frequent
building practice in the middle of the nineteenth century and not
necessarily a sham or a cost-cutting device. Fortunately, the wood
columns were not replaced with stone replicas, nor should they be in
the future. To do so would destroy a great deal of the nineteenth-
century authenticity of Old Capitol. Only the bases of the columns

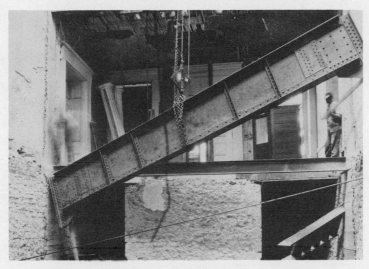

23. Installing steel beams, first-floor hall looking west, 1922.
Original Doric columns in hall in rear.
Old Capitol Reconstruction Album.

in the cupola were replaced because of the rotted condition of the wood. The columns' shafts and capitals are the original ones.

An eye-catching modification on Old Capitol's exterior was the gilding of the copper roof on the dome of the cupola. A workman who laid the gold leaf on the rounded surface was quoted as saying that "the original plans in the erection of the building called for gold on the dome, but until now nothing but paint has been used."[8] His remark about the original plans seems questionable, however, since it was not common practice to gild domes of state capitols at that time. The application of gold leaf in the renovation project required more than 6,400 three-inch square pieces of gold, each square less than one two-thousandths of an inch in thickness. A total of 57,000 square inches of gold leaf was applied in the process, and the cost was slightly less than $200.

The framework of the building also needed reinforcement, and the major vertical supports and horizontal wooden beams were replaced with steel (fig. 23). Other beams that had been constructed

24. *Original lintel and brick construction over*
Supreme Court door to west hall.
Photo Don Roberts, University Photo Service.

with mortise-and-tenon joints were reinforced with handwrought iron clamps. Most of the lintels over doors and windows were left in place because they were still in good condition and bore the 1840s ax marks on their surfaces. One of these is visible under glass in the north hall of the first floor (fig. 24).

As reconstruction work progressed in the 1920s, many Iowa citizens were eager to have souvenirs of Old Capitol. Quite a few obtained portions of the old beams and made them into small footstools or containers to hold metal ashtrays. Walnut balusters from the original spiral staircase became candlestick holders.

Although a west portico for the capitol building had never been constructed because of lack of funds, there was no question that it had been a part of John F. Rague's original design. A 1921 photograph of the west side shows clearly the steps, porch, pediment, and recessed cornice ready to receive a portico (fig. 25). The A. A. Smith report on the renovation indicated that there was some hesitation, even then, concerning the expenditure of money required

25. West facade before addition of portico, 1921.
North Hall visible at left.
Old Capitol Reconstruction Album.

for the portico. But it was thought advisable to go ahead and build it rather than to "be obliged to cut into the new slate roof later on." The four Doric columns of the portico were made by the same process that was used for the original ones on the east portico.

Over the years, the steps of the east entrance had been badly worn by the footsteps of legislators, faculty, and students, and it had been necessary to cover them with wooden planks. The renovation project called for their replacement with long-wearing granite. When all the steps were removed, workers discovered that there was no foundation underneath them and nothing but loose stone under the entire east entrance construction. The stonework of the whole area had to be removed, taken down piece by piece and numbered, and a new foundation was built with the stones replaced in their original location.

No wonder Smith said that "there seemed to be no stopping place in this work, for each part had such a vital connection with the rest of the building that there was no leaving-off place."[9] Nor could the renovation stop with the building alone. It caused concerns for landscaping to surface again, and a decision was made to create a terrace area west of Old Capitol. Proudfoot, Bird, and Rawson were asked to develop a plan for the area between the Physics Building (now MacLean Hall) and the soon-to-be-constructed University Hall (Jessup Hall) that would eliminate the unsightly terrain there. Their recommendation was accepted, and the terrace was completed in the late 1920s (fig. 26).

Interior Changes

The interior rehabilitation of Old Capitol included removal of all the plastering. Much of the early plastering was of poor quality, and the walls were both badly cracked and very irregular because of patching throughout the years. This no doubt meant that the "elegant fresco work" of the late 1850s was completely destroyed. There were, however, some additions to the original decor. Highly decorative plaster cornices, composed of modillions of acanthus

26. West terrace, late 1920s.
Courtesy University of Iowa Archives.

leaves and scrolls alternating with coffered squares, were installed at the intersection of the walls and ceilings in the two large second-floor rooms, the House and Senate chambers. They may have been inspired by widespread interest in the Rockefeller Foundation's re-creation of Colonial Williamsburg in Virginia during the 1920s. A nationwide revival of eighteenth-century design occurred then because of that mammoth reconstruction project.

Old Capitol's original plaster ceilings had been covered with a beaded wood surface at some early date. They were replaced with a plastered ceiling on metal lath throughout the building, a process that made them fireproof and permitted the use of oak flooring on the first- and second-floor levels above them.[10]

The removal of the old plastering made it difficult, if not impossible, to save the original white-pine millwork around doors and windows, and it was completely removed and replaced. A report to President Jessup, presumably by J. M. Fisk, University architect, or A. A. Smith, included the following comment concerning the woodwork:

It [the millwork] had been nailed together with old fashion, [*sic*] large headed cut nails and during the long years of use, had become badly bruised and the cost to remove the many coats of old paint, patch and putty the old holes, would at best leave a very unsatisfactory surface to finish over for a permanent job.[11]

The estimated cost of new millwork was $4,750.

An often-unnoticed characteristic of the millwork around the doors and windows is the slight tapering of the vertical elements of the framework. A drama critic from New York, who visited the campus soon after the 1920s rehabilitation, wrote of the beauty of Old Capitol and commented upon the second-floor chambers. They were, he said, "Georgian in style, with an odd and delightful touch of the Empire in the Egyptian slant to the tall entrance door frames, the tops being four to five inches narrower than the bottom."[12] Early interior photographs show the tapering of the original millwork, and it is not unexpected in Rague's work. He was trained in Greek Classical design and was aware of the Egyptian Revival in the East, and he used such elements in the Dubuque County Jail he designed in 1856. Besides their characteristic tapering, the vertical members of both doors and windows feature projecting "dogears" on both sides.

Except for the office of President Jessup, the entire interior of Old Capitol, both the plaster and millwork, was painted white. The walls of the president's office in the southeast corner of the first floor were paneled with Iowa black walnut about two-thirds of the way up, and the remainder was painted a pale brown color. The painting of the walls and millwork on the first and second floors of Old Capitol was done under the supervision of C. A. Cumming, professor and head of the University Art Department.[13] He had been appointed by President Jessup to select the colors used in the building.

As rehabilitation workers removed the interior millwork over the first-floor entrance doors, they made an exciting discovery—two rectangular stones with incised legends. Concealed behind the broad pine doorframe above the east door was the wording (fig. 27):

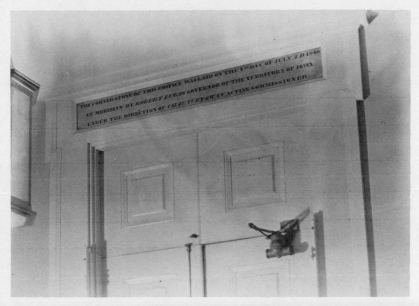

27. Inscription over east door.
Courtesy University of Iowa Archives.

THE CORNERSTONE OF THIS EDIFICE WAS LAID ON THE 4TH DAY
OF JULY, A.D., 1840, AT MERIDIAN BY ROBERT LUCAS, GOV. OF
THE TERRITORY OF IOWA, UNDER THE DIRECTION OF CHAUNCEY
SWAN, ACTING COMMISSIONER

The inscription over the west door read:

JOHN TYLER	E. P. UNUM	JOHN CHAMBERS
Pres^t of the U.S.	1841	Gov. of Iowa

The stones had probably been covered by University authorities at
some time to counteract the impact of the governmental building
upon the faculty and students. But since their discovery, the inscriptions have been left uncovered for public viewing.

The original floors were of plain oak laid upon oak joists. Later,
yellow-pine flooring had been placed over the oak floors in an
effort to level them. During the rehabilitation, new oak floors were
laid in the various rooms of the building, but in the halls on all

three levels terrazzo was installed because of its long-wearing quality.

To make the basement of Old Capitol more usable, the floor level, which had never been finished and was composed of the bare earth, was lowered about eighteen inches.[14] The rooms were divided much as intended in the original plan, although some were subdivided. The new floor was of reinforced concrete with the long north–south hall and the central rotunda surrounding the staircase of terrazzo. The southeast and southwest rooms were assigned to Robert E. Rienow, dean of men, and they were a vast improvement over his previous temporary quarters that had been partitioned off from the west end of the first-floor hall. Adelaide L. Burge, dean of women, moved into the northwest-corner room, and the superintendent of buildings and grounds was in the northeast room.

The settling of Old Capitol over the years had affected the spiral staircase between the first and second floors. There were complaints that it swayed, and it required an additional step to level it. Moreover, some individuals considered the staircase poorly designed or constructed because the original newel posts at the first-floor level were not of the same height; the north one was a full ten inches shorter than the south one (fig. 28). A. A. Smith's description of the original staircase explains this unusual feature of Old Capitol:

Old Capitol Spiral Stairs

As far as we have been able to determine, there is no other spiral stairway with a reverse curve.

In a spiral stairs always turning in the same direction, each step is a part of a "skew arch" and is relatively self-supporting.

The interesting part of this stair construction where the direction of the curve changes is the hand rail. A few words of explanation will be of interest:

Starting from the top, the inner rail is steep, for the steps are narrow on that side. Likewise the outer rail is less steep. The risers are uniform, but the treads vary. In a true spiral

*28. Original spiral staircase from the east, showing left
newel post ten inches higher than the right one, the ribbing
on the underside of the staircase, and the railings on
either side of the basement staircase, 1921.*

Old Capitol Reconstruction Album.

stairs these two rails would continue on the same grade, and would at all times be the same height above the steps. The newel posts at the bottom would also be the same elevation. In these stairs the direction of curving changes near the bottom from a curve to the left to a curve to the right, and the grade of the inside rail becomes less steep; the outer rail more steep.

If the rail followed the same height above the steps in all cases, there would be a "hump" in the south rail and a "sag" in the north rail. This would occur about seven steps from the bottom. To overcome this abrupt change, the inner rail has to be flattened out further up the stairs, and likewise the outer rail needs to be steepened.

In the original stairway, the builder was not able to do this, and he neither succeeded sufficiently in raising the north rail at the bottom, nor in lowering the south rail, so that the original newel posts at the bottom were not of the same height. The north post was 10" shorter than the south one. To my knowledge the effect was not far from right since no one ever noticed this error or difference in height.

In the new rail we succeeded in so grading the two rails that the newel posts at the bottom are of the same elevation. This was done by gradually changing these rail grades, starting from the very top of the stairs.

We have always believed that the inability of the original builder to accomplish the result of getting the newel posts the same height was a fortunate error, as the deception was perfect.

Perhaps if the north post was a little shorter than its companion, it would be more satisfying. Perhaps.

> A. A. Smith
> Superintendent of Grounds
> and Buildings
> State University of Iowa [15]

The original stairs and the area beneath it at the first-floor level differed from the replacements of the 1920s. As Smith indicated, he, Fisk, and those working with them were able to construct the stairs so that both newel posts were of the same height. Walter Siechert, one of the carpenters working on the project from 1922 to 1923, told of several revealing events in a 1971 interview.

Siechert stated that he "drew the details for the stairs but not the plan" and that he "developed a full-size pattern for the curvature of the staircase on a floor in the building."[16] During the 1970s restoration, this pattern was found under the carpet on the oak floor of the House chamber, near the north interior wall and east of the center of the room. Because the floor in that area of the chamber was required for a traffic lane, Siechert's drawing is no longer visible, but it was photographed for historic interest.[17] Siechert also told of planning the details of the new stairs connecting the first floor and the basement.

Besides his planning work, Siechert contributed finishing details to the spiral staircase. He reported that the walnut handrails were put in place "in the square" and that he shaped them while they were in position with a draw-knife he had designed (fig. 29). No two of the walnut balusters in the 1920s staircase are of the same length.

Some details of the original staircase were omitted in the 1920s rehabilitation. One was the wooden ribbed paneling on the underside of the staircase, which had accentuated the beauty of the graceful curve of the stairs. This omission was due to a change in the shape of the landing at the second-floor level that, according to architects today, also changed the shape of the curve at the top. Instead of a considerably larger top step that tapered broadly toward the House chamber at the south, the top step was truncated and turned only to the east—or straight ahead.

In the original construction, the well-hole at the first-floor level was rectangular in form and surrounded by a simple painted-wood balustrade (fig. 30). It contained a straight staircase to the basement that began at the north end of the opening on the first floor and extended downward. In the 1920s, the well-hole was changed to a circular form to complement the staircase, and new spiral stairs to the ground floor beginning on the west and directly under the main staircase were designed and installed.

Slender, tapering octagonal columns supported the original main

29. *Framework for rebuilt staircase with railings*
"in the square," 1922.
Old Capitol Reconstruction Album.

30. Original spiral staircase from the west, 1922.
Old Capitol Reconstruction Album.

staircase, presumably to control the sway. These were not used with the 1920s staircase, but because of observations that the stairs "moved," supports were once again installed, this time of iron pipes. A spiral is considered a self-supporting form, but to date authorities have not approved removing the distracting pipes to determine whether or not their support is really necessary.

The beautiful staircase is considered unusual, if not unique, by many who view it (fig. 31). It is termed a "reverse" spiral because it curves initially to the left at the first-floor level. Some architects say that since more spiral staircases curve initially to the right Old Capitol's main staircase may be considered rare. Walter Siechert disagrees, however, and says that its unique aspect is that it "ends up on the second floor exactly above where it started on the first floor."[18] And it does—the top step is directly over the bottom one.

In addition to the eye-catching staircases, Old Capitol's first- and second-floor halls feature pine columns that define a vestibule area. Doric on the first floor and Corinthian on the second, they are thought to be original with the building. They are pictured frequently in the 1920s rehabilitation photographs, at times lying on

31. *Spiral staircase as rebuilt, c. 1924.*
Courtesy University of Iowa Archives.

32. Corinthian capital and column details from the temple of Lysicrates, plate 43, The Beauties of Modern Architecture, *Minard Lafever, 1835.*

Photo Craig Kohl, University Photo Service.

*33. Corinthian capital and column
by John F. Rague, second-floor hall.*
Photo Don Roberts, University Photo Service.

the floor. They appear to have been placed aside for safekeeping while the demolition was going on around them. The Corinthian capitals are identical to Minard Lafever's drawing of a capital "from the Monument of Lysicrates" in *The Beauties of Modern Architecture.*[19] Since Rague had worked with Lafever, probably in the late 1820s, these columns may have been a part of his original design for the capitol (figs. 32 and 33).[20]

The changes in Old Capitol during the rehabilitation of the 1920s were doubtless more numerous than the legislators who authorized the funds had anticipated. Judging from Smith's observation that one area of repair led to another and "there seemed to be no stopping," University officials must have been equally surprised by the magnitude of the project. Except for the limestone walls, part of the cupola and east portico, and the Doric and Corinthian columns in the main halls, little remained of the original structure. Yet when the rehabilitation was completed, the exterior of Old Capitol appeared almost as it had in 1857 when the University acquired the building.

Furnishings

A refurbished building demanded new furniture, and a large quantity of solid black-walnut furniture was purchased. There were single and double desks, desk chairs, and bookcases for offices, as well as armchairs, side chairs, and long conference tables for use in the House and Senate chambers. All of the chairs, a total of 302, were manufactured by the Milwaukee Chair Company, and the desks, tables, and small case pieces came from the Leopold Desk Company of Burlington. The president of the Leopold Company advised the secretary of the University that the walnut wood used "was grown on Iowa soil and manufactured in Iowa mills." This furniture remains in the Senate chamber today. Three Old Capitol administrative offices at the south end of the ground floor contain many of the desks and chairs of the 1920s, and some of the chairs are used in the public information office at the north end.

A major change in the president's office, which had been occupied by twelve University presidents beginning with Silas Totten in 1860, was the complete remodeling of the fireplace on the south wall. A mantel was removed, and walnut paneling with gold and white Italian marble facing was installed around the fireplace opening, along with a hearth composed of tiles of the same marble. Brass andirons and fender complemented the decor. The fireplace, however, was no longer functional—the chimney was closed and a gas log placed in the fireplace opening. The desk and chairs were identical to the black-walnut furniture used elsewhere in Old Capitol with one exception. The president, Walter Jessup, received one of only two single desks purchased. Where the second single desk was used is not known, but all other occupants of the building were required to share a double desk, perhaps with a secretary or another official, judging from the number of double desks that were purchased and that still exist.

34. Senate chamber chandelier.
Photo Don Roberts, University Photo Service.

Spectacular additions to the House and Senate chambers were the large crystal and brass chandeliers installed in the center of each room (fig. 34). Each chandelier weighed about 650 pounds and supported 1,000 crystal pendants and balls, including 750 prisms. The design of the chandeliers came from eighteenth-century sources and matched that of wall sconces placed between window and door openings around the two rooms. They were purchased from the Bailey-Reynolds Chandelier Company of Kansas City, Missouri, and were installed by a Des Moines electrician who had been given special instructions for uncrating and installing them. He was the only individual permitted to undertake the delicate task. To facilitate cleaning, a winch was placed in the attic area above the ceiling in each room to permit the chandelier to be lowered to the floor.

Other lighting fixtures in the offices were of a hanging-globe type, except the one placed in the president's office. It was a six-arm brass chandelier decorated with crystal pendants. Light in the halls came from brass lantern fixtures with frosted glass panels embossed with clear grape and leaf designs.

Venetian blinds were used as window treatments throughout Old Capitol. They replaced the louvered inside shutters of the early twentieth century. The only carpeting used was the taupe-colored Wilton carpeting manufactured in Philadelphia. It was laid in the president's office and the board room on the first floor and in the two former legislative chambers upstairs.

The furnishings reflected the taste of President Jessup, who apparently served as his own interior designer. He selected all the office and chamber room furniture for the building as well as the kind and color of the carpeting used throughout.

The rehabilitated Old Capitol was praised by an editorial writer for the *Des Moines Register* in early 1928 as "a fine thing both for the university and the whole state." He continued:

> The state's money has not been spent of late years for anything more worth while [sic] in the long run than this restoration.
>
> The fact is that no American can go through an Indepen-

dence hall or an old Iowa state capitol, if it be well preserved, without an effect equivalent to that produced by hearing a really persuasive oration on patriotism. . . . The average human being thinks better and more proudly of the past when he stands in the presence of the past's true monuments.[21]

4. The Architectural Restoration, 1970–1976

A growing University of Iowa demanded space—space not only for classrooms and faculty offices but also for administrative officials. When the 1920s rehabilitation of Old Capitol was completed and the building was reoccupied in 1924, four departments with eighteen officials and staff members were housed there. By 1968, nearly half a century later, the administration had grown dramatically. Thirty individuals—including the president, the vice president for academic affairs and dean of faculties, the vice president for research and dean of the Graduate College, the vice president of planning and development, the dean of academic affairs, and all their assistants and secretaries—were crowded into ten offices in Old Capitol. Two additional vice presidents and their staffs were located inconveniently elsewhere on the campus, and communications were difficult at best. Moreover, since Old Capitol was a recognized historic Iowa landmark, tourists often crowded the halls, impeding movement from one office to another.

Clearly, additional and more efficient space was required. In 1968 Howard R. Bowen, University president from 1964 to 1969, reluctantly proposed that a portion of the old Senate chamber on the second floor and the first-floor board room be partitioned into offices. At least one member of Bowen's staff, the vice president for academic affairs and dean of faculties, was opposed to such a move, believing that it would violate the historic and esthetic integrity of Old Capitol. That individual was Willard L. (Sandy) Boyd, soon to become the University's fifteenth president.

Boyd recalls vividly his despondent reaction to the board of regents' approval of Bowen's proposal at their Des Moines meeting. On the long trip home to Iowa City, he thought about the changes to be made. He also remembers reading the news in the morning paper the next day—the regents had reconsidered their decision after University officials had left and refused to give approval to Bowen's proposal.[1] The two rooms, the Senate chamber and the board room, were to be preserved as they had been rehabilitated in the 1920s. Administrative offices would have to be found outside of Old Capitol.

Boyd inherited Bowen's difficult space problem when he became president in the fall of 1969. Ever since his own office had been located in Old Capitol in 1964 in a portion of the former Supreme Court chamber, he had developed a strong sense of the building's history and its impact upon contemporary state and University problems. With the help of his wife, Susan Kuehn Boyd, he had returned his office to a nineteenth-century appearance, using several outstanding pieces of furniture. Among them was the large desk that had been used in that quadrant of the building by the secretary of the University from 1864 to 1902. Boyd also used a caned swivel office chair, a leather-topped desk-table, and a large secretary. Copies of early Iowa City maps and University photographs completed the decor.

Decision to Restore

On a spring vacation trip in March 1970, the Boyd family visited the old Illinois State Capitol in Springfield, which had been restored and reopened in 1968. Here was a midwestern capitol considered worthy of restoration, a building of the same time period as Iowa's Old Capitol and even designed by the same architect. They had to ask the question, why not restore "our" Old Capitol?

After their return to Iowa, the idea continued to grow. Boyd contacted Susan Hancher and received her encouragement. She agreed to chair a committee of Iowans to plan and carry out the restoration.

On July 18, 1970, the official announcement was made that Old Capitol would be restored. A number of University administrative offices, those of the president and the provost, would soon move to remodeled quarters in nearby Jessup Hall. Boyd stated that "Old Capitol is such an important part of Iowa's heritage that it should be available to future generations in its original form, or as closely to it as possible."[2] He authorized the formation of an advisory committee of University students, alumni, faculty, administrators, and friends to oversee the project. He also asked me to direct the research that would guide Old Capitol's restoration.

A threefold challenge faced the restoration committee when we met for the first time in the board room of Old Capitol on October 3, 1970. What period or periods should the building be restored to, and what would need to be done? How much would it cost and how could it be financed? And finally, how would the building be used once it was restored? The committee members expressed great enthusiasm and support for the project and offered many suggestions for implementing Boyd's idea.

By the second meeting the following November 21, the committee had made two basic decisions that would determine the six-year course of the restoration. First, Old Capitol would be restored to reflect its total history—its territorial, state, and University years. Second, the building would be a "living museum," with some rooms of historical furnishings and exhibits but others for continuing University traditions and functions. The restoration costs could not really be determined since they would depend upon research findings.

Early Research

When President Boyd appointed me to research the interior appearance of Old Capitol throughout its history, I enlisted students from the Department of Home Economics to help me with the project. In September 1970, four of them began to study archival materials, searching for clues to the problem and receiving academic credit for doing so. They studied primarily the early newspapers of Burlington and Iowa City and the Iowa territorial and state official publications prior to 1858—the various House and Senate (Council) journals, the *Laws of Iowa,* and the 1851 *Code of Iowa.*

On December 5, 1970, the restoration committee visited the old Illinois State Capitol in Springfield and studied its restoration. During the day's conferences, the restorers of the Springfield building impressed upon all of us the importance of a well-documented, authentic restoration. We began to realize that Old Capitol's restoration would be a much larger and more demanding undertaking than any of us had initially anticipated.

Despite diligent research efforts and the following up of endless clues, we did not discover the original interior architecture and furnishings, nor did we unearth the original floor plans. One possible clue to the whereabouts of the plans came from an 1840 newspaper article. It stated that among the items placed in the copper box in the cornerstone were "Plans for the Capitol." Because our search for those original plans had so far been fruitless, the Old Capitol Restoration Committee requested and received permission to remove the building's southeast cornerstone, which had "1840" cut into it.

We prepared for the event meticulously and consulted a Chicago paper-preservation specialist about proper handling of the plans once they were removed from the box. We drew a large group of interested spectators, and representatives of newspapers and area radio and television stations covered the removal of the huge stone. Imagine their disappointment—not to mention ours—when the stone proved to be completely solid. There was no copper box, nor even a cavity in which one could have been placed. This was one of many dead ends in the research process.

Months later, a discovery was made in the 1880 board of trustees' records that the secretary of the University had been directed to "cause to cut on the cornerstone of each University building the date of its erection or laying of such cornerstone."[3] The location of Old Capitol's symbolic cornerstone was apparently not known then either; they too had been fooled and the year carved in the wrong stone. However, when the 1920s rehabilitation was undertaken, the cornerstone must have been found, for building superintendent Smith wrote in his account of the remodeling process, "And the box is where you'll find it."[4] He too chose to preserve the secret hiding place of the real cornerstone.

No other attempts to locate the cornerstone containing the copper box were made because further research produced a description of the intended plans for the capitol in the 1840 House *Journal*. A legislative committee had been sent to Iowa City from Burlington to examine the new capitol and report on its progress. The following is an excerpt from their report about Rague's plans:

> . . . the basement story is entered by two doors in the opposite ends, both opening into a hall seven feet wide, which runs directly through the building north and south, dividing it into two equal parts. There are four rooms on each side about twenty feet square, designed for committee rooms. There is also a large and convenient wood-room and a fire-proof vault, arched with brick, and covered with grouted masonry, more than three feet thick, for the safety of public documents. On the next floor there is the same division north and south, and a broad hall or vestibule east and west, entered from the porticos on each side of the building. North of the vestibule, east side, is a room forty-three by twenty-two and a half feet, designed for the supreme court; a corresponding room of the same size on the south of the vestibule, is designed for the use of the Secretary of the Territory. West of the north and south hall are four rooms, equal in size, designed for the use of the Governor, Auditor, Treasurer, and the Library. On the upper floor the north and south hall is omitted. In the south wing is the Representatives hall, fifty-two by forty-three in the clear. In the north wing are the Council Chamber and three small committee rooms, cut off from the west of it.[5]

The committee report was a key discovery for returning Old Capitol to its original interior plan. The major unanswered question was whether Swan and succeeding building superintendents had followed the *intended* plan. This was not resolved until several years later when the needed evidence was found in the walls behind the removed plaster. A second question concerned the rooms on the west side of the first floor. Did the writer list the intended rooms left to right?

Almost from the beginning, the restoration had been viewed as a University project for the U.S. Bicentennial, and that meant completion by 1976. But historical research is by nature a slow, painstaking process, and other than the committee report of the plans, no major clues had been found to document Old Capitol's appearance in the 1840s and 1850s. To move the research process along more quickly, I was granted a leave-of-absence from my teaching duties in the Department of Home Economics for second semester 1970–1971. My first effort was to go to Springfield, Illinois, to study the organization and procedures that had been followed in restoring Rague's capitol there.

From February 8 through 10, 1971, I spent my time wandering through the Illinois capitol. I observed the techniques used in restoring the rooms to reflect the chosen time period, the years during which Abraham Lincoln was governor of Illinois. I noted such details as the square mitered angles in stovepipes at the point where vertical and horizontal pipes joined and the lack of a collar around the pipes where they entered the wall. I asked about the use of pegged wide floor boards and received an apologetic explanation: "They're not right; floors were not made this way during the second quarter of the nineteenth century; we 'inherited' this mistake when we came into the project sometime after it was started. Don't *you* make the same mistake!"

I recorded voluminous notes from my conferences with Lowell Anderson, historic sites curator for the Illinois Historical Society. He advised us to "take pictures like mad" during the entire process. This would be especially important during the removal of walls, plaster, millwork, *anything*. Once something was replaced or covered, the evidence would be lost. Plaster lines on brick often provide a clue to the position of something, a staircase perhaps. Wood plugs set into stone or brick may reveal the location of a wainscot, for example, and often important clues are concealed behind baseboards. Every layer of paint must be checked for the

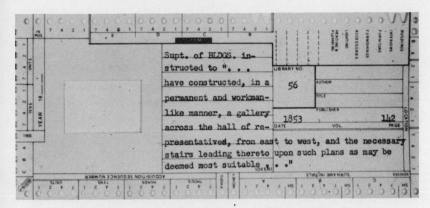

35. *Key-Sort program card concerning construction of*
House chamber gallery.

colors used. Carpet tacks in floorboard layers must be examined
for bits of wool fuzz that may reveal the colors of early carpeting.
The detective aspect of "what walls, floors, and ceilings may tell"
was intriguing.

Anderson provided helpful, detailed information about how to
organize research findings. He had chosen the Key-Sort method
and had developed a program card for recording individual items
about a building—its design, construction, furnishings, activities,
anything that told of the structure's history. Two advantages of the
Key-Sort method stood out: it could be housed in the researcher's
office and thus be immediately accessible, and it offered a high degree of flexibility in the kinds of information it could supply. For
example, the total picture of a single room could be extracted
quickly, or all information on a single phase of the entire building,
such as floor treatments, could be found. The Illinois capitol was
the first building to be programmed by this method, and the Iowa
capitol would soon be the second (fig. 35).

Anderson also gave me generous advice about acquiring and accessioning antique furniture and other large and small items. I
learned both his methods for furnishing rooms and his procedures
for organizing educational slide shows. It was especially helpful to

have the bibliography he developed during the Illinois restoration process.

Later in 1971, I visited a second state capitol, the North Carolina capitol in Raleigh, which had been constructed in the 1830s and was being restored. Again I took copious notes, observing and recording the similarities and differences.

As I began to comprehend the total scope of the restoration project, I was all but overwhelmed by the knowledge (coupled with the lack of knowledge!) of the steps to be taken in the years ahead. More than ever, I realized that I had never restored anything, let alone a distinguished state capitol—and neither had anyone else directly involved with the project, including the University architect. Nevertheless, I wanted to persevere.

One bit of advice from Anderson—that purchase vouchers for construction items and furnishings were the single most important clues in recreating the appearance of the restored Illinois capitol— encouraged me to push further in my search for documentary evidence. Few such vouchers for the building of the Iowa capitol had so far been found in the libraries of the State Historical Society of Iowa in Iowa City and the Department of History and Archives in Des Moines. The thought occurred to me that, because the capitol had initially been funded by the federal government during territorial days, the National Archives in Washington, D.C., probably would contain primary manuscripts about the building. I spent a week there in April 1971, studying at both the Archives and the Library of Congress. The first four days of search produced nothing and were most discouraging, but on the fifth day the archivist helping me located an 1839 letter from the secretary of the Iowa Territory to the secretary of the United States Treasury. In it was a request for "a tabular account of the expenditures of the Territory." Did such an account exist? The archivist was assigned the job of searching for the account. He prudently advised me not to hold my breath but said that he would be in contact as soon as there was something to report.

Three months later a letter from the head archivist at the National Archives arrived at Old Capitol. It stated that, indeed, there *were* territorial accounts—2,347 pages of them—and that at least part of them were directly connected with constructing and furnishing the capitol. A check for $234.70 for photocopying was sent, and once again the waiting began. On December 15, 1971, three large boxes arrived, containing the anticipated gold mine of information. Steven K. Dawson, a graduate assistant on the project, gave up his Christmas vacation to read the manuscripts we received. The territorial accounts provided invaluable information and guided us in many details as the project progressed.

Mysteries Solved and Questions Answered

In the summer of 1972, plaster removal from the walls and ceiling of the House chamber began. It was a step in the process that could either confirm or deny the researchers' educated guesses about the original structure.

One of the major unanswered questions was whether a gallery had been built in the House chamber as originally planned. No physical evidence of such a structure had been found, and there were no pictures of one or references to its removal by the University. Yet both Steve Dawson, the project assistant, and I strongly believed that the original plans had been followed and that a gallery must have been constructed.

Dawson reviewed many historical documents for information that became the basis for his Master of Arts thesis, "The Interior Design of the House of Representatives Chamber of Iowa's Old Capitol 1842–1857." He found many clues to support his belief about the gallery. One was an 1853 legislative act instructing the building superintendent to move ahead with installation of the gallery in the House chamber. A second reference to a gallery was found in an 1854 Iowa City newspaper. The article indicated that at the inauguration of Governor James W. Grimes in the House chamber the "seats, lobbies, and gallery were filled with members, privileged outsiders, great aspirants, and little aspirants."[6] That same year, a shortage of spittoons caused concern on the part of the representatives for the condition of the House gallery floor, and an argument ensued over the proper floor covering: "Mr. Bonson moved that the clerk be authorized to carpet the Gallery of the Hall"; "Mr. Neal moved that the clerk be directed to cover the floor with sawdust"; after some discussion, a substitute motion specifying "cheap carpet" as the floor covering was offered and adopted.[7]

In 1856 another Iowa City newspaper published an announcement concerning a public meeting in the House chamber for ratification of nominations made by the Republican National Convention at Philadelphia. Included was the statement that "The Gallery Will Be Reserved for Ladies."[8] Another reference to the gallery appeared in the House *Journal* of 1856: "And when there are no vacant seats in the Lobby [the area under the gallery] the spectators [will] be required to retire to the Gallery, unless it is already full."[9]

These and other similar clues convinced us that a gallery must have been built in the House chamber as instructed. However, since Benjamin F. Shambaugh had stated unequivocally that galleries had never been constructed because of lack of money, the question still existed.[10] We went one step further in developing our case for the existence of a gallery, consulting an 1853 Webster's dictionary to be sure that the word *gallery* was defined then as it is in twentieth-century thinking. The citation for an interior gallery read "a floor elevated on columns and furnished with pews or seats, usually ranged on three sides of the edifice."[11] Thus the mid-nineteenth-century and the twentieth-century conceptions of a gallery were identical. Surely it was safe, we thought, to project a gallery in plans for restoring the House chamber.

In August 1972, conclusive evidence of the existence of the House gallery was discovered. Behind the plaster, anchor holes that had held its large supporting beams were uncovered between the first and second windows from the wall separating the chamber from the central hall (fig. 36). Also, in the interior brick wall were found bricks positioned vertically, indicating the location of joists that had supported the gallery floor. The gallery *had* existed, and

36. Gallery sockets on east wall of House chamber.

Steve Dawson and I were vindicated. By the time this discovery was made, Dawson had completed his graduate degree and had moved to Minneapolis. When I telephoned him with the news, he reacted with great joy and then said, "You're making me homesick!" I could only reply, "I'm sorry to do that—but I just wanted you to know that your research *was* sound."

While the discovery of the gallery was the single most exciting "find" in the walls, the confirmation of the original floor plan on the first floor was also an important revelation. Because of vertical rows of bricks inserted into the stone walls from the interior, we knew that the four rooms on the west side of the first floor had been built as planned. And conversely, the absence of bricks in the west stone wall of the Senate chamber indicated that the three committee rooms had not been "cut off from the west side of it."

Another unanswered question was how Old Capitol had been heated. It was resolved when we discovered that two nineteenth-century methods—fireplaces and wood-burning stoves—had been used. Workers removing plaster in the first-floor board room came

*37. North wall of Supreme Court chamber showing fireplace with two
stovepipe openings above, uncovered during
the 1970s restoration, 1973.*

upon a bricked-up fireplace opening on the north wall of that
room. Later they found identical evidence in the governor's office
and the Supreme Court chamber. In each instance, however, two
stovepipe holes were also uncovered, placed eight to ten feet above
the fireplace opening (fig. 37). Why would the building have been
heated by both fireplaces and stoves? And why were there *two*
stovepipe holes above each fireplace for two different sizes of pipe?
We reasoned that fireplaces had become unfashionable as a method
of heating by the 1840s. The fact that no fireplaces were ever constructed on the second floor (which was, of course, later construction than the first floor) supported our hypothesis. Only single
stovepipe holes entering the chimneys were found there. Clearly,
at some time the fireplaces had been closed with brick, and stoves
had succeeded fireplaces in supplying heat to the first floor. The
explanation for the existence of two stovepipe holes probably was
related to the University's later use of the building and the division
of spaces into more rooms.

Another question concerned the method of heating the halls. We found our answer when bricked-up stovepipe holes were discovered in the interior brick walls between the north and south halls and the adjacent rooms. These indicated that stovepipes had been carried a great distance from the chimneys—across windows and through the interior walls—into those halls. Also, the auditor's and treasurer's offices had no fireplaces, but each had a single stovepipe hole leading to the chimneys near the cupola, which had been visible in 1853 photographs. Strangely enough, no openings into these chimneys were made into the main east–west halls, so there had been no stoves there. At some time these interior chimneys had been made unusable by filling the shafts with concrete.

A 1906 photograph of the law classroom in the former House chamber shows a beaded wainscot beneath a chair rail that encircled the room (fig. 38). Wood plugs found in the stone and brick walls revealed the exact placement of this decorative feature. Also visible in the photograph are louvered shutters that had replaced the early solid-panel ones.

38. Law class lecture room (House chamber), 1906.
The Hawkeye, *president's office, Old Capitol.*

Still other discoveries about the original building concerned its timber framework. Over each window and door, the 1920s rehabilitation workers had carefully preserved the original hand-hewn lintels, each of which bears the marks of the craftsman's axe. All the doors and windows are rectangular openings, but above each is a carefully built arch of bricks over the lintel. This was a common method of keeping the weight of the wall above from bearing on the lintel and deflecting it to the sides of the opening (see fig. 24).

Funding

Despite the lack of definitive information, the restoration committee accepted recommendations for restoring specific rooms at its third meeting in July 1971. The first priority was the House chamber, and the next in order were the governor's office, the Supreme Court chamber, and the library. The estimated cost of restoring the four rooms was $600,000.

The official fund-raising campaign, to be conducted under the auspices of the University of Iowa Foundation and the University of Iowa Alumni Association, had not yet started, but behind-the-scenes action was occurring. The board of regents officially endorsed the restoration of Old Capitol on October 15, 1971. They supported a drive to secure private funds and an application for appropriate federal funds. They would also support a request for state funds "if needed to complete this important task." Soon after their endorsement, the University of Iowa received the largest gift in its 125-year history.

In the board room of Old Capitol on November 15, 1971, Governor Robert D. Ray, regents president Stanley Redeker, University of Iowa Foundation president C. M. Stanley, and President Willard L. Boyd accepted a $3.5 million donation from Roy and Lucille Carver of Muscatine to the University of Iowa. Many University projects received support from the large gift, and restoration of the House chamber was included for a total of $250,000. The proverbial seed money had been found.

In 1972 Old Capitol was placed on the National Register of Historic Places, a designation that recognized both the building's history and architecture. It also established our eligibility to apply for federal funds to support the restoration project. At this time, the University administration and the restoration committee decided to restore the entire first and second floors, not just the House chamber, and the budget grew to $1,150,700. It was clear that additional private funding would be needed.

A unique fund-raising tactic was to use the building itself. A part of the plaster removed from the House chamber in 1972 was the heavy cornice composed of modillions decorated with acanthus leaves alternating with coffered squares. The University declared these "salvage," and the committee decided to sell them for $25 apiece. Eighty-six modillions were sold, adding $2,150 to the restoration fund.

By the November 1972 committee meeting, we had received word of a grant to the project by the United States Department of Housing and Urban Development. The Open Spaces Program for Historic Preservation awarded the University $313,660 for its commitment to maintain green spaces adjacent to Iowa City's downtown, which at the time had an urban-renewal program in progress. We received another grant from the National Park Service of the United States Department of the Interior for $54,498 to purchase original furniture for the building. Both federal grants required matching funds.

The Old Capitol Schoolchildren's Program was established under the leadership of Abigail Van Allen. She designed the new program to correlate with Iowa history units taught at the fifth-grade level, to provide information concerning Old Capitol's role in Iowa history, and to stimulate interest in its restoration. In promoting the program, Van Allen's committee contacted all the public schools in Iowa, and 497 grades in 105 schools from 80 communities participated. Many Iowa youngsters carried out fund-raising projects, including bake sales, babysitting, designing stationery, and selling "spook insurance" for Halloween. Each child who participated received a poster featuring a story about Old Capitol's history written by Mary Kay Phelan and also a drawing of Old Capitol and the central campus by Eleanor Pownall

*39. University of Iowa campus drawing from
"Legend of a Landmark."*
Courtesy Eleanor Pownall Simmons.
Photo Don Roberts, University Photo Service.

Simmons (fig. 39). The children are recognized in a listing of participating schools that has been placed in the reception area of Old Capitol.

Additional funding to match the federal grants came from the Iowa American Revolution Bicentennial Association. The association provided $5,000 for historic books and furnishings for the territorial–state library and $10,400 for audiovisual systems to interpret the building's history to visitors.

Fund-raising in the private sector began in the fall of 1972 and continued through the spring and summer of 1973. The first of eleven campaign-kickoff dinners was held in Davenport, and others followed in Cedar Rapids, Iowa City, Muscatine, Waterloo, Burlington, Mason City, Fort Dodge, Carroll, Des Moines, and the Spencer–Lake Okoboji area. Those who attended responded enthusiastically to the staff and committee members' presentations about the restoration and the need for funding, and the project received half of the final budget of $1,598,000 in private gifts. In addition to the Carver donation, major gifts included $25,000 from the John Deere Foundation, $20,000 from the Howard and Margaret Hall Foundation to restore the governor's office, and $20,000 from Mr. and Mrs. Peter Bezanson for the Supreme Court chamber. One hundred ninety-four gifts of $1,000 or more were made, and a total of 2,527 people donated to the project. All major donors are recognized on the Iowa Heritage Roll of Honor, and the names of all contributors are included in a permanent record, both of which are on display in the reception area in Old Capitol.

Until early 1974, the Old Capitol Restoration Committee had not requested funding from the state of Iowa. At that time, however, workers removing plaster discovered major structural problems in the walls and roof of the building. These included deteriorated masonry and mortar in some areas of the exterior walls, severe cracking and warping in ceiling beams and roof trusses, and weather-weakened braces in the cupola. They were problems that had to be corrected before other phases of the project could proceed. In addition, the committee wanted to install flameproofing and smoke-detection systems for safety reasons as well as an interior elevator and exterior entrance ramp to make the building accessible to all persons.

Governor Robert Ray offered his support of the request for state funds:

> Old Capitol's situation is understandable and is of a nature that those involved in the restoration would have had difficulty in anticipating.
>
> Old Capitol is a part of our Iowa heritage. We must preserve it, and those who have been deeply involved in this enterprise deserve the appreciation of all Iowans interested in historic preservation.[12]

Ray's comments pointed out the uncertainty of a restoration process—what is hidden in the walls, ceilings, and floors cannot be known until it is exposed. The legislature authorized an appropriation of $330,000, the only funds from the state of Iowa used for the restoration project.

Construction Milestones

When they had secured the initial funding for the House chamber restoration, the University administration and the restoration committee moved quickly. In the summer of 1972, all furniture was removed from the room and the carpet was taken up. The massive chandelier and matching sconces were taken down and meticulously crated. Then the workers began to remove plaster from the north wall. Moisture condensation and seepage through the limestone exterior had caused serious cracking and breaking in the plaster, and it was beyond simple repair. The workers worked by hand, using chisels and hammers, so that no clues behind the plaster would go unobserved.

Meanwhile, the restoration committee contracted with the Springfield, Illinois, architectural firm of Ferry and Henderson, Inc., the same firm that had directed the restoration of Rague's Illinois capitol. The agreement authorized Ferry and Henderson to develop preliminary plans for the House chamber and to submit quotations on doing the working drawings for that room. Later, the firm was contracted for the entire project.

In July 1973, Earl W. Henderson, Jr., the architect, presented a restoration time schedule to begin construction in February 1974 and complete it by December 1975. He included plans for introducing twentieth-century systems of air conditioning, lighting, and temperature and humidity control into the nineteenth-century structure. Such systems would be concealed behind cornices and baseboards, following an ingenious plan devised for the Illinois capitol.

Throughout the succeeding winter, Henderson drafted the final architectural blueprints, and on April 12, 1974, the University advertised for bids on the total project. The bids were opened on May 10, 1974, and were considered favorable to undertaking the entire project. Ten days later the board of regents approved the final construction budget of $1,598,000 and awarded the restoration contract to an Iowa City firm, the Viggo M. Jensen company.

Henderson's plan called for removing the 1920s staircase from first to second floor and replacing it with a replication of the original staircase (see fig. 28). I had agreed that this would produce the only authentic restoration of the hall, which had been designated as an 1842–1857 room. It would also provide visitors a view of the work of mid-nineteenth-century craftsmen rather than that of the

1920s reconstruction. They would see an example of the workers' abilities and their limitations as well, particularly as shown by the discrepancy in the height of the two newel posts at the first-floor level. Other committee members, however, opposed replacing the existing staircase. The University administration consulted many individuals, including members of the board of regents. Most people strongly recommended that, because of the general admiration for the existing staircase and its symbolism to generations of University alumni, the 1920s staircase be retained. The committee voted to keep the existing staircase, and I was the only one who abstained in the final voting. Sentiment had prevailed. The staircase was then load-tested using concrete blocks and was found safe for the anticipated use.

Before replastering began, all the walls were furred out by evening up the stone walls with mortar and the brick ones with fiberglass blocbond. Then wood lath was put up so that the millwork and metal lath could be applied over it. By late 1974, the walls on the first and second floors had been replastered, all by hand.

The missing gallery was also installed, and this time steel beams were used instead of wood. The size of the gallery was the only detail known, and it was based upon the location of the original anchor holes and the position of the joists. Other details were derived from panels used elsewhere in the building, and the octagonal posts beneath the gallery were copied from columns that had supported the original spiral staircase (see fig. 30). Two challenges in designing the gallery were fitting the staircases at either end into the space available for them and planning their appearance. The main spiral staircase became the prototype for the details, and this time the architects were able to include ribbing on the underside (fig. 40).

The interior shutters for each of the forty-five windows arrived in panels the approximate length of the window opening. Each was carefully cut and hung, since no two windows are exactly the same size.

Another time-consuming job was the removal of the 1920s terrazzo flooring in the first- and second-floor halls. Workers used

40. Construction of west staircase to House chamber gallery:
Dave Bush, left, and Jim Shalla, right, 1975.
Old Capitol Photo File.

pneumatic drills, and dust and debris filled all three levels of the building for weeks. Appropriate oak flooring was installed later to reproduce the nineteenth-century prototype.

The huge walnut beams that had been notched and joined together over 146 years ago to support the building's roof were reinforced by the addition of steel members placed parallel to the original beams. The original joists from which the second floor ceilings are suspended were paralleled by similar supports. The fabric of the nineteenth-century construction was thus strengthened by twentieth-century building techniques.

The construction work on Old Capitol was finally completed in October 1975—two months ahead of schedule.

5. The Interior

The problems the committee encountered in restoring the original floor plan and interior architecture of Old Capitol were multitudinous and challenging; those we faced in re-creating the original appearance of the individual rooms were downright overwhelming. We wanted to depict the capitol as it would have appeared in daily use from 1842 to 1857, and yet nothing that could be considered an original piece of furniture or accessory was known to exist. Nor could we deny an even more discouraging fact—no interior photographs or drawings were available.

We knew from the minutes of Old Settlers' Association meetings that the entire contents of the building had been loaded onto oxcarts and bobsleds in November 1857 for the move to Des Moines. When storms developed during the trip, the vehicles became hopelessly mired in snow and mud, probably in Jasper County, and were left to rot. No one knew whether any of the original furnishings had reached Des Moines, but a search of the present state capitol there produced nothing that could be positively identified. Apparently, no inventory of the contents of the Iowa City capitol had been made prior to the move to Des Moines. At least, none appears in official state documents, and there is no evidence of such a record elsewhere. The only thing that can be documented is the arrival of the vault containing state funds, accompanied by the state treasurer.

We were literally starting with *nothing* on this major portion of the restoration.

Researching the Furnishings

The restoration committee wanted Old Capitol's rooms to look the way they had in the territorial and early statehood years. We wanted to give visitors the impression that the officials and legislators had just stepped out for lunch and would soon return to their duties. But without guidance from primary sources, we would have to rely on general assumptions to determine the character of the interior. We knew, for example, that migrating people tend to create buildings that are familiar—and therefore secure—and to furnish them with whatever they had brought with them. This suggested that certain rooms, particularly offices, could have had a domestic appearance because of furniture brought from home.

We could at least, then, turn to the furniture available for purchase during the first half of the nineteenth century to dictate the overall character of the interiors. Books, magazines, and newspapers of the time provided plenty of written and visual evidence of typical furnishings that could have been selected for the capitol. The popular design styles for the restoration period were the American Empire (Late Federal) and the Gothic Revival (Early Victorian). It was also possible that the French-inspired Rococo Revival, which was beginning to be fashionable in the eastern part of the country in the 1850s, could have had an influence. And of course, furniture and accessories predating the building's construction—some as old as 1800, perhaps—could have been brought in by officials.

But the question remained—just what did the interior of Old Capitol look like in the 1840s and 1850s? We continued to search for written descriptions, in letters perhaps, and photographs or sketches of the interior—for any primary source information on which to base an authentic restoration. We started, as we had done earlier when researching the building's architecture and construction, by studying the official territorial and state documents, the journals of the House of Representatives and the Senate (Council), the *Laws of Iowa*, and the 1851 *Code of Iowa*. We also reviewed Iowa City newspapers published during that time period.

Our early findings were fragmentary and incomplete. Appropriations for expenditures might read "To Charles Gaymon for chairs, one hundred and six dollars and fifty cents" or "To Anson Hart for stoves, stove pipes, spittoons, &c., one hundred and sixteen dollars and ninety-five cents."[1] The primary source documentation showed that specific items had been purchased for the building but gave no clues about design styles, materials, colors, and textures, nor were there any indications of where items were to be used. Plans for restoration could hardly be made without that kind of information.

Also, the uses of some Old Capitol rooms were unclear. A notation reading "Joint Resolution, to authorize the Clerk, of the Supreme Court to use a certain room in the Capitol for the purpose of a Clerk's Office"[2] showed that a clerk was assigned an office, but we could not determine its location from the description—and therefore we could not plan a clerk's office.

At one point, we discovered that bills had been paid for transporting the furnishings used in the Burlington capitol to Iowa City in 1842. We realized then that we would have to examine journals and newspapers dating from the beginning of the territory (1838) to determine what had been used in Burlington and, therefore, what would have been moved. There were several newspapers in the early territorial days, and we made several trips to Burlington to study holdings at the library there.

Piece by piece, the puzzle of the appearance of the rooms was beginning to come together, but we did not have enough pieces to complete the picture.

The trips I made to Springfield and Raleigh were helpful, since I saw firsthand what furnishings were included in capitol buildings contemporary with Old Capitol. I studied all the furniture as well as the selection and placement of items on desk surfaces, such as clay pipes, lighting devices, and writing equipment. I noticed that the armchairs used in the Senate chambers of both capitols were identical, and the staff explained that they had been unable to locate any original chairs for the Illinois Senate chamber. In order to provide authenticity for the design of a Senate chair of the time, they had used the North Carolina chair as a prototype for reproductions.

Despite the lack of information concerning Old Capitol's appearance during the 1842 to 1857 restoration period—or perhaps because of it—we began to develop a logical approach to the problem of furnishings. Our first preference was to furnish the building with original furniture and accessories. Second, we would use appropriate antiques of the time period to supplement whatever original items we could find. Finally, we would probably need to replicate both original and antique pieces, especially those needed in multiples.

A furnishings priority listing also helped us organize our efforts. We would complete the House chamber first and then the governor's office, the Supreme Court chamber, the library, and other offices in that order. Our lowest priority was to introduce curtains and draperies throughout the building. Although original vouchers indicated that appropriate fabrics had been purchased, we did not consider draperies essential to the appearance of the rooms. Since inside wood shutters were to be installed at each window, they could be used to control light when needed.

Original furniture was our top priority in furnishing the Old Capitol rooms, and the search for such items was intriguing. It made detectives of us all.

House Chamber Chair

Two important clues concerning the original chairs used in the House chamber appeared in a voucher from the National Archives' holdings. On April 15, 1839, "Twenty Six Cane Chairs" had been purchased from a St. Louis firm for $104 (fig. 41).[3] The use of the single descriptive adjective *cane* told us something about the appearance of the chairs, although the wood they were made of was not mentioned. Many chairs in the Illinois and North Carolina capitol buildings were also caned.

The purchase of twenty-six of anything was puzzling. Usually chairs are purchased singly or by fives, tens, or twelves—but why twenty-six? We researched the number of representatives in 1839 and discovered that there were twenty-six of them. And because

41. *Voucher for purchase of furniture, 1839.*
Courtesy National Archives, Washington, D.C.

the furniture from the Burlington capitol had been transferred to Iowa City, we could assume that the twenty-six representatives at the first session of the legislature in 1842 sat in the caned chairs that had been used in Burlington.

Some time earlier, President Boyd had discovered a walnut armchair with a caned back and seat in a basement room of Old Capitol. We determined that it was of mid-nineteenth-century vintage and wondered if it could be one of the original twenty-six. Its design and construction were correct for the time period, but no documentation was available. We decided that it could serve as a prototype for replication if an original could not be found (fig. 42).

Our continued research at the University archives soon burst that balloon. In a 1921 letter to Walter Jessup (president from 1916 to 1934), a former Iowa City resident asked about the old chair,

42. *Walnut armchair found in basement of Old Capitol and
thought to have been used by Amos Dean,
first president of the University of Iowa.*

noting that it had been the property of the first University president in the late 1850s. Had the University purchased the chair for Amos Dean's use during his infrequent trips to Iowa—or could it possibly have been left behind when furniture was moved to Des Moines? There was certainly no conclusive evidence to support its use in the House chamber.

By mid-1974, we had still not discovered an original House chamber chair. We agreed, then, to design one, based upon the Illinois and North Carolina chairs and on secondary sources of information, including Thomas H. Ormsbee's line drawings.[4] One of the chairs in Ormsbee's book on Early American furniture was similar to the chairs in the other capitols we studied, although its parts were somewhat thicker and heavier. Moreover, printed comments indicated that such a chair often was caned. We reasoned that since the territory west of the Mississippi River was indeed frontier country, the basic form of the chair could have been used without the refinements that characterize similar chairs produced in the East. Ann M. Baker, a graduate assistant, prepared working drawings for a chair, and the restoration committee approved her design for use in replication.

Final blueprints for the chair were being processed when fate— or chance—intervened. A University employee who had worked on removing plaster from the walls of the building came to my office and handed me an announcement of an auction to be held two days later on August 1, 1974 (fig. 43). One of the offerings was a "Walnut Arm Chair (from the Old State Capitol in Iowa City)."

By this time, of course, I was skeptical when I heard of "original" furniture. Given their design and construction, many of the items that I had examined could not possibly have been in the building during the 1842 to 1857 period. But the hunt intrigued me, and that afternoon I went to the site of the auction, the nearby town of What Cheer, and examined the chair.

The walnut chair was similar to the one Baker had designed, although it was not as graceful and some of its parts were thicker. It had holes for caning concealed under its upholstery, and it showed evidence of construction methods used between 1830 and 1850. It

PUBLIC AUCTION

1½ Miles North of What Cheer, Iowa, on Highway 21

Thursday, Aug. 1, 1974

5:30 P.M.

Notice — Evening Sale

— ANTIQUES —

Thomas. A. Edison Amberola (Cylinder Record Player), Pat. Date 1896; 30 Cylinder Records; 6-Volt Radio; Brunswick Record Player; Lots of Records; Combination Book Case & China Cabinet; Sellers Kitchen Cabinet; Oak Dresser; Baby Cradle; Oak Drop Leaf Dining Table; 5 Oak Chairs; Maple Wash Stand with Mirror and Towel Rack; <u>Walnut Arm Chair (from the Old State Capital in Iowa City)</u>; Bowl and Pitcher Set; Wall Telephone; Cradle Phone; Large Trunk; Lard Press; 2 Copper Boilers; Small Iron Kettle; Stomper Butter Churn; Glass Butter Churn; 3 Lanterns; Scales; Conservo Cooker; Tin Boxes; Bottle Capper; 2 five-gallon Cream Cans; White Glass Aladdin Lamp; 'Guardian Hand Gun (American Model 1878); Maytag Sausage Grinder; Food Grinder (Pat. Date 1887); 2 Quart Milk Bottles; Cream Top With Face; Iron Car; Dinner Bell; Buggy Whip Stand; Several Kerosene Lamps; 2 Iron Beds; and Many Antiques Not Listed.

— HOUSEHOLD GOODS —

Avocado Gas Range; Dining Table; 5 Straight Chairs and Host Chair; Buffet; Bedroom Suite; Metal Bed Complete; Dresser; Metal Wardrobe; Small Super Flame Oil Burner; Allen Oil Burner; Speed Queen Washing Machine (Like New); Singer Sewing Machine with Electric Attachments; Coffee Table; Book Shelf; Corner Stand; 4 Odd Chairs; Crocks; Starlight Skelgas Dryer; Mangle Electric Ironer; Combination Radio and Record Player; 3-piece Sectional.

More Furniture By Sale Date

— MISCELLANEOUS ITEMS —

12-ft. Polar Craft Aluminum Boat; Oars; Champion 5⅝ Horse Motor; 6½" Utility Saw; ½" Speedway Electric Drill (Life New); 9½' x 11' Tarpaulin; Paint Sprayer; 2 Wash Tubs; Well Pipe Jack.

Terms — Cash   Not Responsible in Case of Accidents

REX STRASSER

AND OTHER CONSIGNERS

Wayne H. Hudson, Auctioneer   Bob Reinert, Clerk

43. Sale bill for What Cheer auction.
Old Capitol Photo File.

also had a stamped notation, "State of Iowa Custodians," identifying it as state property. The only historical information concerning the chair was that the owner had purchased it at a state surplus sale in Des Moines some years previously. It seemed possible that it was one of the "Twenty Six Cane Chairs."

I asked to buy the chair before the sale, but that was not permitted since it was considered a major attraction for the auction. So I returned two days later, filled with apprehension that someone might outbid me, even though I had been authorized to bid whatever was needed to buy the chair. I had only one rival, though, and I bought the chair for $90, just $14 less than all twenty-six original chairs had cost in 1839. In fact, the price I paid was a favorable price on the 1974 antique market.

Subsequent newspaper articles concerning our find produced additional armchairs from many locations throughout the State— Indianola, Menlo, Des Moines, Sigourney, even Iowa City, and others. All could be traced to the Des Moines capitol and had been made available for sale as state surplus. The earlier history of the chairs could not be verified, and only secondhand information connected them to Old Capitol. Nevertheless, we considered the chair appropriate for a frontier capitol of the time. The earlier blueprints were shelved and new ones were made based upon our discovery. In all, eleven of the armchairs were found. We also discovered that side chairs matching the armchairs had existed, and we were able to obtain two. A matching swivel desk chair was later donated to the project.

At last a reasonable solution to one major problem had developed. Although our chair design was based upon secondary sources, the design and construction of chairs used in furnishing capitols of the time appeared to confirm its use in the Iowa capitol. To date, a documented original has not been found.

Bidding documents were written with specifications tightly drawn for all aspects of building the chairs—materials, construction, and finish. The first armchair had been made entirely of walnut, but subsequent ones used oak, butternut, and cherry in addition to walnut. In some chairs, two or three woods were combined. For replicating the chairs, we decided to use walnut only. It was a common wood for Iowa furniture of the period because of the extensive walnut groves in the eastern part of the state.

None of the armchairs we found had a caned seat, but each one had a seat of upholstery covering the original cane holes. None of the chair backs had cane holes, but each was upholstered to match the seat. Often the wood surrounding the upholstered back was different from the remainder of the frame, suggesting that that part of the chair had been replaced. We wondered whether an original caned back frame had been removed. In the end, using the Illinois and North Carolina chairs as examples, we decided to have the backs and seats of the replicated chairs caned. And since research showed that armchairs of the time were made with three different treatments—back and seat caned; back and seat upholstered, preferably in leather; back upholstered and seat caned—we restored the eleven chairs we had acquired using all three methods.

When the bids for the replications were advertised, there was considerable interest in manufacturing these chairs. We required hand-construction methods using mortise-and-tenon joints and a specific French polish finish used during the time period in Iowa. The latter was the determining factor in our awarding the contract to the Norman Schanz Company of West Amana, a firm that continues to use that hand-applied and hand-rubbed finish (fig. 44).

House Chamber Desk

The search for an original House chamber desk was equally long and frustrating. By 1975 not a single desk had been found. Once again we decided to use Ann Baker's designs, one for a single desk and one for a double desk, as patterns for replication.

Twenty-four hours before the bid for manufacturing the desks was to be let, surprising news arrived in a letter from a former Des Moines resident living in Florida, Paul R. Beall. An old schoolmate, Rudolph F. Wertsch, had written to Beall, telling of the Old Capitol restoration and the search for original furniture. Wertsch

44. Replications of House Chamber chair and desk
made by Norman Schanz Company, Amana.
A portion of House chamber carpet shows in detail.
Old Capitol Photo File.

had asked Beall if he still had "that nice little desk" that he had
been told was from Iowa's first state capitol. Beall had the desk
and indicated that he was willing to lend it to the University so that
replicas could be made. He had inherited it from his grandfather
who had been given the desk by Iowa state officials.

In his letter, Beall included pictures of a single desk not unlike
the one Baker had designed. We stopped the bidding process immediately and telephoned Beall, requesting to have the desk
crated and shipped to Iowa City by air freight because time was of
essence. Then we awaited its arrival eagerly and anxiously. A call
from the Chicago airport informed us that it had arrived there but
could not be sent on because the air carriers serving the Cedar
Rapids–Iowa City airport did not have a hold sufficiently large for

the crate. The University moving crew and a truck were dispatched in short order. The desk was returned to Old Capitol from Florida by airplane and truck, 118 years after it had left by oxcart for Des Moines.

Researchers analyzed the walnut desk carefully and agreed that it could well have been a part of the original furniture, perhaps one of the desks made by Evan Evans in Burlington in 1839.[5] The only part that was not original was the desk top, where formica had replaced the original materials.

The restoration committee drafted and advertised new bidding documents based upon the Beall desk. The low bidder was an Illinois firm, which was confident of its ability to meet the specifications. Several weeks later, though, the president of the company called to request specific information about the desired French polish finish. When we contacted Norman Schanz, he explained that the formula and process were a secret of the Amana cabinetmakers and could not be shared. Aware that they could not meet the terms of the contract, the Illinois firm withdrew, and the bidding on the desks was reopened. This time the Schanz firm was successful.

After publicity concerning the discovery of the desk, a second one was located—just seventy miles away! It belonged to Grinnell College and had been given to Josiah B. Grinnell, who had served as a state senator in Old Capitol in the 1850s. The two desks were identical except for one major difference. The tops of both desks were wedge-shaped, but the left side of the Beall desk tapered inward from front to back while the right side of the Grinnell desk was the one that tapered. Also, each desk was slightly curved at both the back and the front of the top surface. These were very important clues to the arrangement of the desks in a semicircle in the chamber.

Fortunately, the Grinnell desk had the original writing surface in place, nineteenth-century grained oilcloth. Replicating this material was difficult since twentieth-century oilcloth is smooth and shiny. We checked dozens of materials for possible use and selected Calabana cloth, an awning material, as the nearest in appearance to the original fabric.

Paul Beall visited Old Capitol several years later and offered to donate his desk, which was then on loan to the project, in exchange for a replica of the original. Because of his great affection for Old Capitol, Norman Schanz made another reproduction and presented it to Beall. His original desk has been placed in the library. The Grinnell desk is on display in the House chamber on a permanent loan agreement with Grinnell College.

One research question remained to trouble us—had double desks ever been used in Old Capitol? We thought they might have been, since they existed in the Illinois and North Carolina capitols, but no hard evidence of their use in Old Capitol had emerged. Several months after the restored building was opened, a double walnut desk—identical in design characteristics and construction to the original single desks—was offered to the restoration. It had been the property of a state senator who served in the 1850s, and it confirmed that this furniture form had been used, at least in the Senate chamber.

Other Original Furnishings

In the library on the south wall is a bank of five tall bookcases, each of which may be original to the building. They came from the holdings of the State Historical Society of Iowa. Since that organization was founded in Old Capitol on January 28, 1857, and occupied rooms there until 1901, they may have been left in the building by the state government at the time of the move to Des Moines. At least their design and construction suggest that possibility. The society donated the bookcases to the restoration.

The society also gave us the original lock for the east door of Old Capitol. It had been presented to the society by the University building superintendent who supervised the 1920s rehabilitation. When I saw the lock, I immediately thought of a large brass key on display in the president's office. When the key was tried in the lock, it fit perfectly. All locks for the building, large and small, were therefore made from that prototype (fig. 45). In addition,

45. Original lock and key to east door.
Old Capitol Photo File.

several tools used in Old Capitol's original construction—a draw knife, a plane, and a ripsaw that had been used in constructing the spiral staircase—were found in the society's collections. These tools, as well as several 8″ × 8″ oak beams that had been removed from the cupola in the 1920s, are now on display in the ground-floor rotunda.

Appropriate Antiques

To compile a list of the antique furniture and accessories needed to re-create the various rooms authentically, we used the items that appeared on original purchase vouchers and others from the rooms of the Illinois and North Carolina capitols. We then sent copies of the list to antique dealers in eastern Iowa and western Illinois. We also gave copies to interested persons on request and to people attending presentations about the proposed restoration. We made

46. Antique walnut secretary from Scott County.
Old Capitol Photo File.

trips to antique shops as well, and we wrote newspaper and magazine articles describing the needs of Old Capitol. The results of our efforts were highly beneficial to the project. The furnishings committee received some items as gifts, purchased others, and rejected still others.

The very first piece of furniture for the restoration was an anonymous gift, a large secretary made of native Iowa black walnut by a Scott County craftsman about 1840 (fig. 46). Other gifts included walnut drop-leaf tables, a walnut stand-up desk, a rocking chair, a 3,100-pound safe, an early, primitive pine-pedestal table, a brass-trimmed rosewood lap desk, and a walnut desk with pigeon holes from the Madison County Courthouse, to name a few.

Among the furnishings purchased were eight Windsor-type benches, two double stand-up desks, several wardrobes, a massive walnut desk-table with an inset leather surface, commode stands for bowl and pitcher sets, and an early nineteenth-century Windsor armchair.

Two large pieces of furniture, a large "speaker's desk" for the House chamber and a judges' bench for the Supreme Court chamber, were designed by the architects and researchers because of the lack of prototypes. These were handmade of walnut by Amana craftsmen at the Schanz factory.

Floor Coverings

Original vouchers from the territorial and statehood periods indicated the purchase of many yards of carpeting. Yet in the many records studied, only two adjectives provided information about the type of carpet used. They were the words *cheap*, for the carpeting in the gallery of the House chamber, and *Venetian*, for other carpeting in an undesignated location. When we researched floor coverings of the restoration period, we found several types— ingrain, Brussels and Wilton carpets, homemade rag-rug strips, and floor cloth—to be typical of the time.

At a 1973 meeting of the Victorian Society in America, I met a

Massachusetts couple, Peter S. and Mary Lou Grinnell, both of whom had Iowa ancestors in their family trees. We had several conversations about Old Capitol, a building familiar to both Grinnells. They told of several pieces of a Brussels carpet of the 1840 to 1850 period that they had found in an antique shop in Vermont, and they offered to lend it for possible use in the project. When the carpet arrived in Iowa City, we analyzed it and thought it would be suitable as a pattern for the House chamber. To ensure its proper replication, the carpet samples were also analyzed by a textile chemist in the Department of Home Economics.

More than one hundred and fifty yards were needed to carpet the House chamber according to dictates of the time. Sue Hancher and I literally became twentieth-century carpetbaggers, carrying the Grinnells' samples to Chicago, New York, and Boston for conferences with representatives of carpet-manufacturing firms. We contacted a total of seventeen companies, and each indicated confidence that it could produce an accurate replication of the Classic Revival design and colors—olive green, crimson, gold, and a delicate peach against a grey–tan background. However, only one firm could guarantee authentic reproduction of the fabric's texture, a low, uncut pile that gave the appearance of needlepoint. That firm, Newbury Carpets of Boston headed by Albert R. Wadsworth, received the bid and drew up exacting specifications for the carpet, which was manufactured in Durham, England.

Four times the carpet sample crossed the Atlantic Ocean by air before we approved the design, dyes, and texture. Because the carpet was custom-designed from the Grinnells' samples at University expense, the University of Iowa owns design rights to the fabric and receives a modest design fee from individuals who wish to use it in restorations.

Examples of other mid-nineteenth-century carpets have also been used in the restored rooms. The governor's office and the library feature large, antique ingrain carpets, and other smaller ingrains are used in the auditor's and treasurer's offices. In the Supreme Court chamber is a long strip of a handmade rag rug of the nineteenth century.

Accessories

Early in the research process, I became aware that books from the original library in Old Capitol had been dispersed throughout the state. We would need the aid of a trained librarian to locate them. The committee appointed a research librarian, Martha Esbin, to study the original book catalogs for the territorial and state libraries and to track down as many as possible of the early collection. She located many of the original books, most of them at the Iowa Department of History and Archives in Des Moines. Discovery of these books was the first indication that anything transported to Des Moines in 1857 other than the treasurer's safe had actually arrived there.

We determined that a book was originally from the territorial–state library by checking its listing in the two catalogs published before 1857. We used two other clues—a publication date of 1857 or before and the words *Iowa State Library* written across the bottom of page thirty of each volume. The *Laws of Iowa* (1855) had required the state librarian to do this as a means of establishing ownership and preventing theft. During the restoration, nearly 1,000 of the original books were returned to Old Capitol. The great majority had pages yellowed with age and torn in many places, and the leather bindings frequently were badly deteriorated and brittle.

Another important accessory—the quill pen—presented a challenge. We wanted to obtain authentic quill pens, since original vouchers supported their use in the statehouse. The committee learned that Lewis Glaser of Charlottesville, Virginia, was the only craftsman still making authentic goose-quill pens in the United States. Glaser's number-one client was the United States Supreme Court, which presents a pair of quills in a polished pewter holder to each attorney who has a case heard by the Court. The demand upon Glaser was high because of the great number of requests for his pens.

Somewhat reluctantly, Glaser agreed to fabricate the pens for the Iowa capitol. Half of the order arrived the morning of July 1,

1976, just in time to be placed on the desks in the House chamber before an opening reception that evening. The remaining quills came a year later. The quills, taken from geese raised in Israel, were personally selected by Glaser. The holders are filled with lead shot to hold the quills erect.

Often the committee had to rely on logical assumptions to determine the answers to questions about the types of furnishings used. We knew from vouchers, for example, that several hundred spittoons were purchased, and yet there were never more than forty to fifty officials and legislators in the capitol at one time. How could they possibly have used so many brass spittoons? We suddenly realized that the cuspidors had probably been made not of brass but of ceramic, and they were always placed on the floor. Of course, they were often kicked over and broken and had to be replaced. All the spittoons we finally used in the restored building are typical of the period—antique Bennington and Bennington-type—except for a single brass one.

We felt that other useful and decorative objects, including maps, were essential in re-creating a "used" look in the restored areas. Documents showed, in fact, that maps of the United States, Iowa, and other states had been purchased. The very first gift-in-kind to the project was an 1839 map entitled "United States and Texas." We have since obtained other Iowa maps dating from 1844 to 1855.

An unusual gift came from the Dwight Conklin family—a reproduction of a twenty-nine-star United States flag, commemorating Iowa's entry into the Union as the twenty-ninth state. The Conklin children raised the money for the flag and its standard by detasseling corn.

Other authentic accessories of the period are now on display in Old Capitol. They include lap desks of the type used by legislators when they traveled, metal document boxes with handles, bowl-and-pitcher sets, sand shakers, and ceramic ink wells.

All in all, the committee was able to assemble a wealth of furnishings and accessories. Eleven students studying interior design in the Department of Home Economics drew on this material to create proposals for plans of rooms in the restored building. Anne

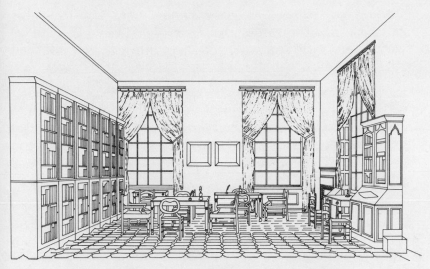

47. Furnishing plan for territorial–state library.
Designed by Anne Current, 1975.
Old Capitol Photo File.

Current's design for the territorial–state library was a part of her Senior Honors' thesis (fig. 47).

Heating

To give visitors evidence of the earliest heating methods in Old Capitol, the committee sought cast-iron stoves and andirons and other equipment for the fireplaces. Our search for antique stoves coincided with the energy crisis of the 1970s, and old ones were all but impossible to find and purchase. Finally, we located a reproduction of an authentic ten-plate stove featuring pointed-arch Gothic Revival panels.

To obtain nine of the stoves at an affordable price, we relied on the family ties of Susan Hancher. Her brother-in-law, a hardware dealer in Sweetwater, Tennessee, volunteered to supply the stoves at a wholesale price, and they were shipped directly to Iowa City from Portland, Maine. They were installed with square-angled stovepipes set into the original stovepipe holes, and they were placed upon shallow platforms made of rows of bricks. Wood boxes containing dry logs were placed conveniently near each stove and fireplace.

The three fireplaces found in the governor's office, the library, and the Supreme Court chamber were restored. The other fireplace, located in the president's office, was left as it was remodeled in the 1920s. Three sets of cast-iron andirons were found for use in fireplaces, but other fireplace utensils of the period are still being sought.

Lighting

Original vouchers told of the purchase of many brass candlesticks for the capitol building. Often they noted that candles should be made of tallow from the sperm whale. The restoration committee purchased forty antique brass candlesticks, many of them of a type that includes a beehive form in the stem. Professional candlemakers in Iowa City made tallow candles as their gift to the restoration, and these are placed in replicated candle boxes hung on the walls for candle storage.

One generous University alumnus gave the project a collection of nineteenth-century lighting devices. It included four Sandwich-glass whale-oil lamps, of which two are now on the speaker's desk in the House chamber and two are on the writing tables in the library. Two other whale-oil lamps with hanging prisms are on the judges' bench in the Supreme Court chamber. There were also several smaller lighting devices and a large Sinumbra lamp, which rests now on the governor's desk. The same alumnus also gave an early nineteenth century Sheraton-style mirror, now hanging over a washstand in the treasurer's office.

An unusual find—two matching whale-oil chandeliers with their original tole finish—resulted from a notice we placed in *The Magazine Antiques* to request information about Old Capitol and its furnishings. A Philadelphia antiques dealer sent a picture and documented the fact that the chandeliers were of the restoration period. They now hang in the Supreme Court chamber.

Twentieth-century lighting, of course, depends upon electricity, and fire codes demand that it be used, even in restorations where bare flames would be more desirable for authenticity and effect. Light switches are not a part of nineteenth-century decor, but they are essential to operating electrified devices. We were able to conceal the light controls in baseboards, a technique developed by the architects when they restored the Illinois capitol. Only one light switch is visible in the restored areas of Old Capitol, a 1920s switch in the president's office.

Supplementary lighting for interior rooms is provided by floodlights on tracks near the ceilings and by lights behind the coved cornice in the House chamber. The halls are lighted by replications of nineteenth-century wall sconces and a six-globe chandelier that hangs over the spiral staircase.

Workers on the Project

Re-creating a structure and authentic furnishings of the second quarter of the nineteenth century in the third quarter of the twentieth was a challenge to the restoration project's workers. An authentic restoration required construction and finishing techniques of the 1840 to 1850 period, and locating artisans who were expert in such methods was paramount.

Harold Brender, foreman of the construction crew, assembled an exceptional group of workers. They had both the needed techniques as well as another important characteristic—they cared about Old Capitol. And they knew that their work would be seen and appreciated by thousands of visitors for years to come. Brender expressed the crew's thinking as follows:

We've never done a job like this before, and we'll probably never do another like it.

Ordinarily, you come back to a building a few weeks after you've finished it and you see nobody respects the work you've put into it.

But everybody's going to come and look at the work we're doing here. That gives you a different feeling. When a person puts in time doing a job, it means something to him to know people are going to respect his craftsmanship.[6]

The workers themselves respected the quality of the materials used in the restoration. They spoke admiringly of the oak flooring and stair treads, the walnut stair railings and spindles, and the perfect-grade, clean white pine of the millwork for windows and doors. All these were essential to reproduce the nineteenth-century appearance of the building's interior.

Jim Shalla, a Kalona carpenter, was assigned the job of fitting the walnut handrails and balusters to the two gallery staircases in the House chamber. He used nine pieces of walnut to form one three-foot section of the rail, which had two double curves. Of this example of fine craftsmanship, Brender said: "No one will ever know how that was done, except the two men who did it."[7]

Another carpenter, Charles Ruppert, commented:

This is one of the most interesting jobs I've been on. I never imagined that I'd be working on the restoration of Old Capitol. I've lived here my entire life, studied the history of the county and, well, this is the most important part of the campus. I'm glad to see that someone finally got around to restoring something around here.[8]

The employees of the cabinet shop in West Amana who reproduced furniture for the House chamber were equally aware of their contribution to Old Capitol's history. Norman Schanz stated:

The way I feel about making these particular chairs is something very special to us because we feel that this is really a one-time affair in Iowa and a once-in-a-lifetime, really.

The way we do it here in the Amanas, of course, is very common to how these chairs were built by hand with mortise and tenon construction. Really, the idea behind it is they were made so they would last, and I think this has proven itself very well in the old chair itself.

And as far as building furniture, this is the way it is still done here and, hopefully, will be for many more years.[9]

Many of the nineteenth-century antiques used in the building were refinished by a Cedar Rapids firm whose members were highly sensitive to the building's heritage. It was a special challenge to fit together the five tall bookcases and make them into one long unit, and they worked meticulously to preserve the old and used appearance of the cases and other original furniture from the building.

When Old Capitol was reopened in 1976, the first people to see the interior were the dedicated workers. On the evening of July 1, special tours were conducted for them, followed by a reception at the home of President and Mrs. Boyd. Eavesdroppers overheard comments that attested to the great pride the workers felt in the finished product—"This is where I worked," "That staircase was a real bearcat," "I didn't think we could do it," and "Isn't it simply beautiful?"

Special Events and Additional Notes

Although all University administrative offices other than the Graduate College offices on the ground floor had been removed from Old Capitol, the restoration staff was granted office space on the first floor. We worked in three offices partitioned off in the former Supreme Court chamber. Tourists came and went in the building and were their own guides as they walked from room to room. Later, as the restoration progressed, the Old Capitol project's offices were moved three times, to the president's office area, to the northeast quadrant of the ground floor, and finally to their permanent location at the south end of the basement.

In March of 1972, a graduate assistant spotted a group of people standing at the west end of the second floor near the timing mechanism that rang the bell in the cupola. Closer observation made it clear that a University student couple was being married there, and to our knowledge it was the first and only wedding to be performed in Old Capitol. We called the president's office in Jessup Hall to inform them of the unusual event, and Mary Parden, longtime administrative assistant to four presidents, commented: "Darn—I always hoped it would be one of us!"

A month later on April 6, 1972, another newsworthy event occurred. The Iowa Supreme Court convened in Old Capitol, the first time that body had heard a case in the building in 115 years. The hearing was held in Old Capitol's Senate chamber in conjunction with the University of Iowa Student Bar Association's annual Supreme Court Day.

During the summer of 1973, the University employee who went up into the cupola every day to raise the United States and State of Iowa flags was stung by a bee. This was not itself a newsworthy report, but when it led to the discovery that Old Capitol had bees in its bonnet, it became front-page news in state newspapers. One of the sixteen columns on the exterior of the tower was completely filled with honey, and the bees were in the process of moving on to a second column. We had to call exterminators in order to preserve the original ornate Corinthian capitals and columns.

As the beginning of the actual restoration approached, we realized that a completed project would be the end result! A celebration would be in order as a way of opening the restored Old Capitol. Susan Hancher appointed Clark Houghton, a member of the restoration committee, to chair a planning subcommittee for the event, and Boyd asked D. C. Spriestersbach, vice president and head of the University's U.S. Bicentennial Committee, to co-chair the new committee. Later, that committee would be known as the "host committee."

Old Capitol was a subject of interest to another researcher, William Seale of Washington, D.C., who with noted architectural historian, Henry-Russell Hitchcock, was writing a book on the extant state capitols in each of the fifty states. Seale visited Old Capitol in August 1973 and expressed great interest and approval of what he saw underway. He shared many of his experiences as a professional restorer with me.

On October 17, 1973, the entire building was closed to the public until the 1976 reopening. Only the Old Capitol Restoration Committee offices remained. The Graduate College offices were moved to newly remodeled space in Gilmore Hall, the former Law Building. At that time Spriestersbach, dean of the Graduate College, gave a party for "a very special lady"—Old Capitol—complete with dozens of long-stemmed red roses. He commented that it was a sad day to be moving from such historic quarters.

Another significant move from the building involved a historic figure. An 8½-foot, 110-pound statue of Samuel J. Kirkwood, Iowa's governor during the War Between the States, had for many years dominated the north end of the transverse hall on the first floor of Old Capitol. A gift in 1927 from an Iowa City citizens' group, it had been cast from the original model of the Vinnie Ream Hoxie statue of Kirkwood, which is in Statuary Hall in the United States Capitol.

Although Kirkwood came to Iowa City in 1855 and had a lumber mill in the Coralville area, his only documented connection with Old Capitol was as a founding member of the Iowa Republican Party, first organized in the building on February 22, 1856. He distinguished himself politically as governor, United States senator, and cabinet officer after Old Capitol's days as a capitol—and elsewhere, in Des Moines and Washington. We thought it inappropriate to keep the Kirkwood statue in the building, since his period of service to the state did not coincide with the designated restoration periods. President Boyd conceived the idea of donating the statue to Kirkwood Community College in Cedar Rapids, where it could be displayed at the school named in his honor, and it was moved there in March 1974.

A very important addition to the Old Capitol staff was made on July 1, 1973, when Bette Thompson was appointed half-time secretary for the restoration project. Fifteen years later—in 1988—she continues to be an indispensable part of the building's management as administrator of Old Capitol programs, supervising and coordinating the office, the volunteer program, the student employees, and the gift-shop personnel.

Student interest in the restoration was high, and as director of research I had requests for experience on the project every semester. In addition to Dawson's and Baker's master's theses, one senior honors' thesis and eleven directed individual study projects were completed (see Appendix B). Because of frequent questions about the hows and whys of the restoration, I developed a university course in historic restoration methodology, which carried credit in both the history and home economics departments. I first offered the course in the spring of 1976 and twenty-one students enrolled. I had help in this venture from history professor Robert D. Dykstra, who lectured on nineteenth-century history, and from architectural historian Robert L. Alexander, who presented his specialty, American architecture of the nineteenth century. Students completing the methodology course could also earn credit by undertaking an internship at Old Capitol. They served as docents and helped us in many ways. In the process, they learned a great deal about the daily operation of a small historic museum and gained experience in office procedures, accessioning, developing displays, recruiting and working with volunteers, and operating the gift shop.

6. The Dedication

The culmination of the six years of restoration of Old Capitol was a four-day celebration July 1–4, 1976, and on July 3 the building was officially opened to the public. The program for the dedication ceremony acknowledges the many people who came together that day to recognize the building's role in Iowa's past, present, and future.

A former University student, then a U.S. State Department official, returned to the campus and performed his student job of raising the flag by hand from the cupola. A Chicano nun presented the invocation. Descendants of the first governor of the Iowa Territory, Robert Lucas, led the large audience in the Pledge of Allegiance. An excerpt from the Declaration of Independence was read by a University student. Simon Estes, a former University student now with the Metropolitan Opera Company of New York, sang the national anthem. An official representing the U.S. Department of State presented a bronze plaque recognizing Old Capitol as a National Historic Landmark. Girl Guides from Durham, England, where the House chamber carpet was made, were coincidentally visiting Iowa at the time of the celebration, and they presented a British flag to Old Capitol on behalf of Her Majesty the Queen. Iowa's governor, Robert D. Ray, spoke of the symbolism of the building then, now, and tomorrow. And a University graduate, a member of the Mesquakie Indian tribe, introduced his father to pronounce the benediction in his native tongue. His words reflected the thoughts Chief Poweshiek had shared 138 years earlier. They commemorated the ties of the native American and the white cultures from the past to the present and augured well for the future:

Today, as we assemble here, let it be known that we are to keep on thinking as one and to remember again what the Creator has planned for us, the reason why we are able to be here at this ceremony.

This location was where they came together for the first time, your people and the Mesquakies, where we purchased the land from the governor on which is now our village in Tama County. This is the only thing I am asking from Him: to give us to understand each other as one and also to pray that we may continue to remind ourselves what He has given us, life, as ever, so be it, as only He, the Creator are we dependent upon and not each other as mortals. But now, as life goes on and as our friendship has long ago been established, we are beginning to go in the opposite direction from one another as people because we may have forgotten the teaching and knowledge left by our ancestors.

Our forefathers had called upon the Creator and their religion in order to permit us to live here in this part of the country, *Iowa,* and our part in this ceremony, my son and I, is to reaffirm the first meeting in this building between our people, and to remember the original Mesquakies who came here to buy the land we now occupy, and to pray to heaven and earth that the friendship between us to be as one, and for continuance and re-affirmation, to the Creator, to help us in this endeavor.

The understanding which comes about at this gathering of our people today is intended so that we may have faith in each and every one of us, so be it. That is all.[1]

Following these words, University president, Willard L. Boyd, presented the building's original key to Governor Ray, who then reopened Old Capitol to the public. It was a historic moment that symbolized both the theme of the dedication weekend—"Old

48. Dedication of the restored Old Capitol, July 3, 1976.
Old Capitol Photo File.

Capitol: Cornerstone of Iowa History—Past, Present, and Future"—and the theme of the University's U.S. Bicentennial celebration—"Iowa '76: Looking Back Toward the Future."

It was indeed a memorable and rewarding day for all who had worked so long, so diligently, and so unselfishly. Throughout the bicentennial weekend, more than 12,000 people signed the guest book and toured Old Capitol (fig. 48). They praised the restoration for its authenticity, its innovation in recapturing three periods of occupancy, and its beauty (figs. 49–59). All seemed to agree that Old Capitol's restoration was a bicentennial project worthy of a great state and a great University, for the histories of the building, the state, and the university were—and still are—inseparable.

49. President's office (1920s period).
Photo Don Roberts, University Photo Service.

50. Governor's office (1842–1857).
Photo Don Roberts, University Photo Service.

51. Auditor's office (1842–1857).
Photo Don Roberts, University Photo Service.

52. Treasurer's office (1842–1857).
Photo Don Roberts, University Photo Service.

53. *Territorial–state library (1842–1857).*
Photo Don Roberts, University Photo Service.

54. *Supreme Court chamber (1842–1857).*
Photo Don Roberts, University Photo Service.

55. First-floor hall and spiral staircase (1920s period).
Photo Don Roberts, University Photo Service.

56. Second-floor hall (1842–1857).
Photo Don Roberts, University Photo Service.

57. Senate chamber (1920s period).
Photo Don Roberts, University Photo Service.

58. *House chamber from gallery level (1842–1857).*
Photo Don Roberts, University Photo Service.

59. *House chamber from main level (1842–1857).*
Photo Don Roberts, University Photo Service.

Epilogue

A restoration can probably never be considered finally completed or finished. Historic facts that had been missed may be discovered—or additional original furniture and accessories may be found—or more appropriate antiques from the restoration period may surface. Additional funding may develop and allow the installation of previously omitted items, such as oak flooring for Old Capitol's ground floor and a major restoration of books in the original library collection. So the history of the building may grow, and its appearance may change.

In the years since the 1976 dedication and grand reopening of Old Capitol, the building has changed measurably—and yet it seems unchanged in spirit.

Interior Changes

Since 1976, there have been many additions of furnishings. To celebrate the first anniversary of the dedication, the Iowa City Antique Dealers' Association sponsored a benefit antique show July 1–3, 1977, at the Iowa Memorial Union. This was the first of several such occasions, and the admission charges were earmarked for the continuing restoration of the building. Among the items we were able to add to the building was a large, geometric ingrain carpet for the governor's office. We used other funds to repair seven of the original armchairs.

In December 1978, an observant visitor to the building questioned a docent about the small metal caps placed at intervals on the walls of the halls. The response was that they covered electrical outlets for nineteenth-century wall sconces to be installed "when we have the funding for them." That same day the interested visitor called me to ask what the cost would be for replicas of the fixtures we wanted. When I told him it would be in the neighborhood of $13,000 he said, "That will be your Christmas present!" We were thus able to order twenty-seven sconces from a historic interior designer and supplier in Pennsylvania, and they were installed in the halls in 1979. The same donor and his wife, who had requested anonymity, later gave $10,000 for a matching six-globe chandelier, which now hangs from the dome over the spiral staircase.

Several armchairs and sidechairs matching the House chamber prototype have also been added to the decor, five of them as gifts. Other pieces of furniture given since the 1976 opening include a rocking chair for the governor's office, two walnut firehouse-Windsor chairs for the Supreme Court chamber, a leather-topped desk-table that was originally in the Dubuque County Courthouse, and a large mirror now placed over the fireplace in the governor's office.

The Iowa chapter of the Daughters of the American Revolution have provided funds for several important additions to the furnishings of Old Capitol. One is a walnut washstand, complete with towel rails, which was placed in the governor's office. The organization also gave a large ingrain rug for the library and a nineteenth-century walnut frame for a lithograph of George Washington.

The unusually large pigeonhole desk in the treasurer's office was discovered by an Iowa City antiques dealer. Its provenance indicates that it had originally been owned by a Roman Catholic priest in Spring Valley, Illinois.

In 1988, based upon research we had undertaken before 1976, we had merino draperies designed, fabricated, and installed in the House chamber. Funding was supplied by a gift to the Old Capitol Endowment Fund by John and Thelma McColm, West Liberty. We plan to add more drapery and curtain treatments as funds allow.

Exterior Improvements

In the fall of 1981 and the spring of 1982, the exterior of Old Capitol was given a facelift, its first in nineteen years. All the exterior wood—on columns, cornices, cupola, window frames, and doors— was sandpainted using the original process. Storm windows were also installed.

For many years the west terrace approach to Old Capitol, which had been completed in 1927, had been deteriorating and was badly in need of major repairs. A grant of $160,000 from interest earned by a large gift to the state of Iowa for historical purposes, the $5,000,000 Herrick Historical Fund, and University funds finally allowed the reconstruction of the imposing terrace in 1983. To produce more serviceable traffic lanes, granite was substituted for brick and concrete for worn limestone. The overgrown plantings were also completely replaced, and benches were installed. The terrace, a favorite relaxing spot for hundreds of students and staff since its original construction, continues to be a pleasant place for study or lunch. The University's master plan for landscaping the Pentacrest area includes new plantings for the east facade and the north and south sides of the building.

Throughout its history, Old Capitol has proudly flown the nation's flag from the pinnacle of its flagstaff. In the mid-1960s, Howard R. Bowen recommended flying the state of Iowa flag immediately below the Stars and Stripes, a practice that has continued since that year. A University tradition of honoring deceased students, faculty, staff, and board of regents members by flying the United States flag at half-mast for a day developed over the years and continues to be followed today.

The revised United States laws of flag etiquette, established in 1976, permit flying the national emblem twenty-four hours daily, provided that it is lighted continuously and that an all-weather flag is flown. James O. Freedman, sixteenth president of the University, endorsed this procedure early in the 1983–1984 academic year, and on September 9, 1983, this practice was introduced at Old Capitol.

Special Events and Additional Notes

In keeping with the restoration committee's directive that Old Capitol be a living museum, many events—traditional and otherwise—have occurred in the building. Moreover, Old Capitol has remained newsworthy.

The University and Old Capitol were both highly honored, for example, when it was announced on October 15, 1977, in Mobile, Alabama, that a student-made film had won the top prize in a national competition sponsored by the National Trust for Historic Preservation. "Old Capitol: Restoration of a Landmark," a University U.S. Bicentennial project, reviewed the history of the building and included both the 1976 opening festivities and a film tour of the restored structure. Franklin Miller, associate professor in the Department of Speech and Dramatic Art produced the twenty-five minute film, and Paul Hopkins, a graduate student, directed, edited, and composed it with the help of several other graduate students. Hopkins received a $1,000 award for his role in the finished project.

Earlier in that same year, a long-standing University tradition was reinstituted in April 1977 when a candidate for the Ph.D. degree in the College of Education successfully defended his doctoral dissertation in the historic Senate chamber. Another University tradition was renewed in 1978 when the bell in the cupola began ringing once again to signal the beginning and ending of class periods. Eight years earlier the practice had been discontinued because of mechanical failure. Early custodians, of course, had rung the bell by hand until an automatic bell-ringing mechanism, a gift of the Class of 1948, was installed in 1950. After that automatic system failed, nearly a generation of University students never heard the sound of the bell and perhaps did not know of its existence. There were thus many surprised expressions at 1:20 P.M. on March 30, 1978, when the tones were heard again, and many looked upward in search of the source. The bell now rings sixteen times at each ringing, for approximately thirty seconds.

On January 29, 1981, the bell was rung continuously for ten

minutes to celebrate the safe return of the American hostages who had been held in Iran for 444 days. Then, in front of Old Capitol's east portico, there was a short service that included words of thanks and distribution of yellow ribbons.

Since the restoration, many groups and organizations have requested permission to meet in Old Capitol. One with historic precedent for such an occasion was the Iowa Supreme Court, which convened in the Supreme Court chamber on October 29, 1976, as a bicentennial project of the Court. They had met in the building in 1972, but this was their first meeting in the court's original quarters in 119 years. They heard the case of a demoted Cedar Rapids detective.

The State Historical Society of Iowa celebrated the 120th anniversary of its founding in 1857 in the room of its birth, the Senate chamber. Five years later the society held a similar event there to recognize 125 years of service to the history of Iowa.

In the same room, on February 27, 1978, a public hearing was held concerning the proposed Equal Rights Amendment to the United States Constitution. Many present—both women and men—signed a petition directed to members of the Iowa legislature encouraging them to support the amendment.

On March 10, 1980, the Senate chamber was the site of the announcement of a major gift to the University to benefit the internationally recognized Writers' Workshop. James A. Michener, distinguished American novelist, gave $500,000 to aid young writers, and the fund was established in his name.

The Senate chamber has also been a frequent meeting site for academic groups, including the University faculty and student senates, the College of Liberal Arts faculty, the Iowa High School Forensic League, the Law and World Hunger Symposium, and the University of Iowa Symposium and Conference on Television Criticism. Even groups of elementary school students have convened there.

Perhaps the most unusual occasion is the performance in Old Capitol of an original play, "The Birth of Iowa City." It has been produced annually in early May in the Senate chamber by second-grade students from Robert Lucas School in Iowa City. Mary Ann Woodburn, a dedicated Old Capitol volunteer, is the teacher who instituted this highly creative learning experience. The play tells the story of the siting of the capital city and the beginnings of Old Capitol. Woodburn's students wrote the script and created the set from large refrigerator boxes. Each year they portray Robert Lucas, John F. Rague, Chauncey Swan, and others.

On one occasion, children from the same class replaced regular tour guides and, aided by their parents and teacher, instructed visitors about the building's history. And on May 16, 1978, Mike Smith, then a Robert Lucas second-grader, was honored as the one-hundred-thousandth visitor to the restored Old Capitol. He received a replica of the original brass key to the building, and his class received an Old Capitol plate to display in their classroom.

National recognition came to Old Capitol in March 1978, when Wendell Garrett, editor and publisher of *The Magazine Antiques*, traveled to Iowa City from New York to tour the building. The magazine's photographer, Arthur Vitols, came with Garrett, and the two men and their wives spent an entire day taking exterior and interior pictures. The pictures were used to illustrate an article I wrote for the July 1978 issue of the magazine.

Also in 1978, the entire four-block Pentacrest was named a National Historic District and entered in the National Register of Historic Places. This designation served to complement Old Capitol's distinction as a National Historic Landmark.

Over the years, many distinguished people have toured the building. Former U.S. Senator John Culver and his family visited in 1977. Iowa's former governor, Robert D. Ray, and his wife have come frequently. In June 1983, Governor Terry E. Branstad, his wife Chris, and their children Eric and Allison also visited Old Capitol as a part of the governor's mini-vacation program to promote tourism in Iowa.

Various events of importance have taken place in the Senate chamber. It was the meeting site for the Midwest Universities' Consortium for International Activities in February 1979. In April of the same year, Northrop Frye, distinguished literary critic and chancellor of Victoria College at the University of Toronto in Canada, delivered a presentation on literary theory. In September 1980, a public lecture was offered by Tasim Olawale Elias, vice president of the International Court of Justice, which had ruled on the Iranian hostage situation earlier that same year. Old Capitol was also the site for the symposium on Cerebral Blood Flow sponsored by the Cardiovascular Center of the College of Medicine (1981), the Plenary Session of the Society of French Historical Studies (1983), and a symposium on educational research for thirty foreign ambassadors hosted by Senator Charles Grassley (1986).

Other events have taken place near Old Capitol's east portico, including performances by the Royal Lichtenstein Circus. It has also been the site of choice for many student events, including the anti-Vietnam war protests of the late 1960s and early 1970s as well as hundreds of pep rallies, which were also held on the west portico. In June 1980, students held an anti-draft rally to oppose the resumption of the military draft, and later that year, on December 13, they kept a vigil for the slain former rock star, John Lennon. The Arab Student Association stood on the east portico in silence in June 1981 to protest Israel's bombing of an Iraqi nuclear reactor and American military aid to Israel. They also held a memorial ceremony for assassinated Egyptian president, Anwar Sadat, in October 1981.

Old Capitol has been the background for more joyous occasions too. Each year since 1914, a corn monument has been erected by students in the College of Engineering to celebrate homecoming weekend. It was first built at the intersection of Clinton Street and Iowa Avenue, but later the site was changed to the west side of Old Capitol, adjacent to the west terrace. It is by now a long-standing University homecoming tradition.

The traditional annual convocation, which marks the beginning of the University's school year each autumn, has also been held near Old Capitol. The ceremony was started on the west portico, was moved to the east portico in 1967, and then was discontinued a year later. The tradition was revived, however, in 1984.

Under the guidance of Bette Thompson, program administrator

at Old Capitol, a strong volunteer program has developed. Women and men from Iowa City and the nearby area, both University students and nonstudents, have served as volunteer docents and gift-shop personnel every day since July 1, 1976. There have been 438 individuals in all. Thirty-three have achieved recognition for contributing over 500 hours, and seven persons have given over 1,000 hours. These dedicated volunteers are listed on a permanent plaque in the reception area. One notable volunteer, Susan Hancher, remained committed to Old Capitol long after completing her work as chair of the restoration committee. For many years she gave two mornings weekly to schedule gift-shop personnel and to compile a record of news articles about events in the building.

A newsletter, appropriately named "The Willing Regiment," is published especially for Old Capitol volunteers. It features news about the building, impressions recorded by volunteers, and short research papers developed by student employees, among other items of interest. Another publication, the "Old Capitol Cookbook," was compiled by four volunteers and produced $4,972.50 for the operation of the building.

Old Capitol continues to draw many visitors and averages twenty to twenty-five thousand people annually. More than one hundred events take place in the Senate chamber each year. Tours for schoolchildren are scheduled each spring and fall, and an average of 100 schoolbuses transport more than 5,000 students to the building annually. Other special tours are arranged for senior citizens, the disadvantaged, and various groups visiting the campus. Tours for foreign visitors are available in German in both printed form and on cassette, and other foreign-language tours are being developed.

My own relationship with Old Capitol has continued, and I have served as director since 1975. Other staff members include Bette Thompson, program administrator; Ann Smothers, secretary; and Harold Wagler, who has served as custodian since the building reopened in 1976. We also have help from a University graduate assistant and several workstudy students.

Willard Boyd, the person who started the restoration project, resigned the presidency of the University in March 1981 to become president of the Field Museum of Natural History in Chicago. In reflecting upon his tenure at Iowa, he stated that the best single moment during his twelve years as president was "the day we opened the restored Old Capitol. That building reflects what this University has been, what it is, and what it can be."

Today, the history of Old Capitol continues to expand with the discovery of more historical facts. New and varied events supplement traditional occasions and enhance the role of the building locally, statewide, and nationally. And if some long-hidden letters of an early legislator describing the wall colors of the building will just turn up in someone's attic, the restoration may be made more complete and authentic. I believe they will!

Appendix A
Old Capitol Restoration Committee

Mrs. Virgil M. (Susan) Hancher, chair
Frank T. Nye, vice-chair
Margaret N. Keyes, director of research

Members of the
Executive Committee

Susan Hancher, chair
Frank T. Nye, vice-chair
Robert L. Alexander
Susan K. Boyd
Willard L. Boyd
Arthur L. Gillis
George L. Horner
H. Clark Houghton
Richard R. Jordison, Sr.
Margaret N. Keyes
Joseph W. Meyer
William Shanhouse
Bette A. Thompson
Darrell D. Wyrick

Members of the
National Committee

Philip D. Adler
Walter A. Anneberg
Barbara Avery
Ann M. Baker
Arabella Bendixen
Francis Braley
Edward Breen
Don Burington
Etna Charlton
W. Charlene Conklin
Anne Current
Allin W. Dakin
David Dancer
W. E. Darrington
Steven K. Dawson
Candice K. Elliott
Edwin B. Green
Kathleen Heninger

Robert T. Hilton
Richard Kautz
Frederick W. Kent
Clifton C. Lamborn
E. F. Lindquist
Kenneth MacDonald
Bruce E. Mahan
Katherine Maring
Phyllis E. Podhajsky
Robert D. Ray
Jonathan Richards
Fred Schwengel
Abigail Van Allen
Percie Van Alstine
William J. Wagner
Ruth Waterman
Floyd F. Whitmore
David Wright

Subcommittees of the National Committee

Acquisitions

Margaret N. Keyes, Ruth
  Waterman, co-chairs
Ann M. Baker
Arabella Bendixen
Susan K. Boyd
Francis Braley
Etna Charlton
Steven K. Dawson
Edwin B. Green
Kathleen Heninger
Joseph W. Meyer
Percie Van Alstine

Finance

Joseph W. Meyer, Darrell D.
  Wyrick, co-chairs
Barbara Avery

Susan K. Boyd
Abigail Van Allen

Legislative Liaison

Frank T. Nye, chair
Edward Breen
W. Charlene Conklin
W. E. Darrington
Clifton C. Lamborn

Library Advisory

Martha Esbin, chair
Dale M. Bentz
James H. Gritton
Frank Paluka

University Furnishings

Robert L. Alexander, chair
Barbara Avery
Edward Breen
Allin W. Dakin
Richard Kautz
Katherine Maring

Members of the Host Committee

H. Clark Houghton,
  Duane C. Spriestersbach,
  co-chairs
Dale M. Bentz
W. Charlene Conklin
Robert N. Downer
Ann M. Feddersen
Gloria Gelman
Susan Hancher, ex-officio
Peter T. Harstad
Loren L. Hickerson
Margaret N. Keyes, ex-officio
Doris Kohn

Mary Jane McLaughlin, ex-officio
Byron R. Ross

Subcommittees of the Host Committee

Facilities and Service

Gloria Gelman, chair
John D. Dooley
Richard E. Gibson
Richard Plastino

Finance

Byron R. Ross, chair
O. D. Bartholow
Ralph Radcliff
Robert M. Sierk

Formal Dedication Ceremony

W. Charlene Conklin, Robert N.
  Downer, co-chairs
Elaine Estes
Richard Graeme
Lida Greene
Carl Hamilton
Richard Kautz
Edward Lucas
Jill McLaughlin
George Mills
Frank T. Nye
Jonathan Richards
Russell Ross
Lola Wearin
Irving Weber

James Wockenfuss
Dean Zenor

Invitations

Dale M. Bentz, chair
Kenneth D. Donelson
Alan L. Swanson

Liaison

Peter T. Harstad, chair
Murray Goodman
Robert Johnson
Jacquelyn McCarthy
Lorraine Mintzmeyer
Marvin Hartwig

Project

Ann M. Feddersen, Doris Kohn,
  co-chairs
Donald C. Bryant
Jean Kendall
Mary Lea Kruse
Charles W. Lindemann
James E. Meeks
Lyle C. Merriman
Frank Seiberling
Nancy Seiberling

Publicity

Loren L. Hickerson, chair
Robert M. Furlong
Don McQuillen
Edward Ryan

Appendix B
University Student Involvement

Graduate Research Assistants

Ann M. Baker
Leslie Bohnenkamp
Pamela Buresh
Steven K. Dawson
Janet Dumbaugh
Anita Frimml
Nancy Kuebler
Christine M. Piotrowski
Phyllis Podhajsky
Kathleen Polvi

*Students Who Conducted
Research for Academic Credit*

Ann M. Baker
Richard Blazek
Anne Current
Sue Corlett
Steven K. Dawson
Condra Sue Easley
Deborah Ginger
Candice K. Goodrich
Pamela Loris
Alecia Pinkham
David W. Wright

Appendix C
Old Capitol Dedication Program

*Concert by the University of
Iowa Brass Quintet*

John Beer, trumpet
John Merriman, trumpet
Paul Anderson, French horn
John Hill, trombone
Robert Yeats, tuba

Program of Dedication

Master of Ceremonies: H. Clark
  Houghton, Iowa City, co-chair
  of the Old Capitol Host
  Committee

*Raising of the flags of the United
States and the State of Iowa:*
  Homer Calkin, diplomatic
  historian, U.S. Department
  of State

The National Anthem: Simon Estes,
  accompanied by the Iowa Brass
  Quintet

Invocation: Sister Irene Munoz,
  Muscatine, Migrant Committee

Pledge to the Flag: Bruce Kendrick
  and Marcy Lucas Patterson,
  descendants of Robert Lucas,
  first governor of the Territory of
  Iowa (1838–1841)

Declaration of Independence
  (excerpt): Steven Bahls,
  graduate of the University
  of Iowa

*Designation of Old Capitol as a
National Historic Landmark:*
  Grant Petersen, superintendent,
  Herbert Hoover National
  Historic Site

Remarks by Mary Louise Petersen,
  president of the Board of
  Regents; introduction of the
  governor

Address: The Honorable Robert
  D. Ray, governor of Iowa

Benediction: Donald Wanatee,
  graduate of the University
  of Iowa

*Presentation to the governor of the
original key to Old Capitol:*

President Willard L. Boyd, the
University of Iowa

Reopening of Old Capitol:
Governor Ray

Band Concert

Summer Town Band of Solon
Alan Stang, conductor

Notes

1. The Territorial and Statehood Years, 1842–1857

1 F. R. Aumann, "Poweshiek," *The Palimpsest*, September 1927, pp. 303–304. The first written evidence of Poweshiek's quotation is to be found at the Manuscripts Division, State Historical Society of Iowa, Iowa City, in the memoirs of M. Etta Cartwright (Coxe) entitled "Poweshiek's Oration and Reminiscences," n.d.

2 *Journal of the House of Representatives of the First Legislative Assembly of the Territory of Iowa* [1838] (Burlington: Clarke and M'Kenny, Printers, 1839), pp. 162–163.

3 Charles Negus, "The Early History of Iowa," *Annals of Iowa*, October 1869, p. 326.

4 "Notice," *Iowa Territorial Gazette and Burlington Advertiser*, Burlington, July 27, 1839, p. 4; "Notice," *Iowa News*, Dubuque, October 12, 1839, p. 4.

5 *Journal of the House of Representatives of the Third Legislative Assembly of the Territory of Iowa* [1840] (Dubuque: Wm. W. Coriell, Printer, 1841), p. 200.

6 *Journal of the House of Representatives of the Second Legislative Assembly of the Territory of Iowa* [1839] (Burlington: Printed by J. Gardner Edwards, 1840), p. 94.

7 Benjamin F. Shambaugh, *The Old Stone Capitol Remembers* (Iowa City: State Historical Society of Iowa, 1939); University of Iowa Archives: Shambaugh Family Papers.

8 "Capitol of Iowa," *Iowa Sun*, Davenport, May 29, 1839, p. 2.

9 *Legislative and Contingent Expenses of the Territory of Iowa*. Account No. 81,586. National Archives, Washington, D.C.

10 Fourth (4th) Territory Assembly, 1841. Bills and Memorials; Claims and Communications. Six 22. State Historical Society of Iowa, Des Moines.

11 Samuel Charles Mazzuchelli, *The Memoirs of Father Samuel Mazzuchelli, O.P.* (Chicago: Priory Press, 1967), p. 239.

12 *Journal of the House of Representatives* in *Journals of the Second Legislative Assembly of the Territory of Iowa, Special Session* [July 13, 1840], pp. 30–31.

13 Editorial, *Burlington Hawk-Eye and Iowa Patriot*, Burlington, July 23, 1840, p. 2.

14 *Journal of the House of Representatives of the Third Legislative Assembly of the Territory of Iowa* [1840], pp. 190–192.

15 *Journal of the House of Representatives of the Fifth Legislative Assembly of the Territory of Iowa* [1842] (Iowa City: William Crum, Printer, 1843), p. 32.

16 *Journal of the Council of the Fifth Legislative Assembly of the Territory of Iowa* [1842] (Davenport: Alfred Sander, Printer, 1843), pp. 214–217.

17 See note 16.

18 *Journal of the House of Representatives of the Sixth Legislative Assembly of the Territory of Iowa* [1843] (Dubuque: Wilson and Keesecker, Printers, 1844), pp. 284–286.

19 *Journal of the House of Representatives of the General Assembly of the State of Iowa* [1846] (Burlington: Printed at the Hawk-Eye Office, 1847), p. 26.

20 *Acts, Resolutions and Memorials Passed at the Regular Session of the Second General Assembly of the State of Iowa* [1848] (Iowa City: Printed by Palmer & Paul, 1849), p. 162.

21 *Acts, Resolutions and Memorials Passed at the Regular Session of the Third General Assembly of the State of Iowa* [1850] (Iowa City: Palmer & Paul, State Printers, 1851), p. 226.

22 *Acts, Resolutions and Memorials Passed at the Regular Session of the Fourth General Assembly of the State of Iowa* [1852] (Iowa City: Wm. H. Merritt, State Printer, 1853), pp. 141–142.

23 "Old Capitol Pillars Over Seventy Years Old, Yet Good as New," *Daily Iowan*, Saturday, October 14, 1922, p. 1. In an interview, Sydell recalled that the cost of material and labor for constructing the four columns in 1852 was $50.

24 "Notes Regarding Building of Old Capitol in Iowa City" from personal recollections of Geo. H. Yewell, December 26, 1922, as recorded by his brother-in-law, Oscar C. Coast. Yewell was an artist who did many studies of Iowa City in the 1840 to 1850 period and observed the capitol under construction.

25 *Contingent Expenses of the Governor of the Territory of Iowa*. Account No. 77,498. National Archives, Washington, D.C., p. 12.

26 Charles Negus, "The Early History of Iowa," *Annals of Iowa*, January 1874, p. 13.

27 *Acts and Resolutions Passed at the First Session of the General Assembly of the State of Iowa* [1846] (Iowa City: A. H. Palmer, Printer, 1847), p. 188.

2. The University Years, 1857–1970

1 Primary sources documenting University use of Old Capitol include records (minutes) of the board of trustees (1847–1870), the board of regents (1870–1909), and the board of education (1910–1970s); minutes of the College of Liberal Arts faculty (1860–1945); and miscellaneous presidential and faculty folders held in the University of Iowa Archives.

2 "The State University–Normal Department," *Iowa City Weekly Republican*, July 13, 1859, p. 1.

3 *Iowa City Republican*, October 16, 1867, p. 3.

4 *Report of the Joint Committee Appointed to Visit the State University and Deaf and Dumb Asylum*, 1866, pp. 1–4.

5 "The Law Department of Iowa State University," *University Reporter*, July 1870, p. 1.

6 "Five Spot Called Weak Name for Iowa Campus; Seek Another," *Daily Iowan*, December 11, 1924; "Now It's 'Pentacrest;' Judges New Name for Old Capitol Campus," *Daily Iowan*, December 19, 1924; Letter to Virgil M. Hancher from E. A. Plank, D.D.S., Independence, Iowa, June 27, 1955, identifying himself as the originator of the word *Pentacrest*.

7 Walter A. Jessup, "A University Soldier's Memorial," *Iowa Alumnus*, January 1919, p. 88.

8 See note 7.

9 John T. Silence, "Local Attorney Rebuilds Campus of 'Gay Nineties' in Memory Picture," *Daily Iowan*, December 11, 1927, p. 8.

10 College of Liberal Arts Faculty minutes, Box 1. Book 1. September 12, 1860, to June 24, 1881. University of Iowa Archives.

3. The Rehabilitation, 1921–1924

1 One set of the 1912 floor plans is held at Old Capitol. A second set is in the University of Iowa Archives. Unfortunately, a University official, considering that "they never would be needed," had many of the blueprints of architectural details destroyed, probably in the 1950 to 1960 period.

2 "The Old Capitol Building: A Plea for Its Preservation," *Iowa Alumnus*, February 1916, pp. 5–8.

3 Definition from the Heritage Conservation and Recreation Service, United States Department of the Interior.

4 A. A. Smith, comp. "Old Capitol Reconstruction Album," December 14, 1936. Typescript with photographs.

   Smith was the University's superintendent of grounds and buildings when the report was completed and was listed as "Superintendent of

Maintenance" during the rehabilitation. Three copies of his report are known to exist. The first copy was presented to the president and later was transferred to the office of the director of Old Capitol. The second is in the University of Iowa Archives, Special Collections, University Library. The third is in the Manuscripts Division of the State Historical Society of Iowa, Iowa City.

The three copies of the report are not identical. Most of the typed material is consistent, although there are some variations and omissions. The photographs vary greatly, making comparison of the three reports essential. All photographs were taken by Fred W. Kent, then director of University Photo Service.

The administrative departments in Old Capitol were titled as follows: Extension Division, Grounds and Buildings, Mailing Room, Multigraph Room, Dean of the College of Liberal Arts, Dean of Men, Alumni Bureau, President, Registrar, Secretary and Treasurer, Finance Committee of Board of Education, Inventory, and Memorial Union. The last three were housed in the same room.

5 "An Act for an appropriation for the fireproofing and preservation of the Old Capitol Building at Iowa City, Iowa," in *Acts and Joint Resolutions Passed at the Regular Session of the Thirty-Seventh General Assembly of the State of Iowa* (Des Moines: State of Iowa, 1917), pp. 273–274.

6 Smith, "Old Capitol Reconstruction Album."

7 Jessup File, 1921–1922, Folder No. 5. Letter from A. A. Smith to Walter A. Jessup, May 8, 1922. University of Iowa Archives.

8 "Entire Dome of Old Capitol to be Given Layer of Gold Leaf," *Daily Iowan*, October 28, 1922, p. 5.

9 Smith, "Old Capitol Reconstruction Album."

10 See note 9.

11 "Summary of the Cost to Complete the Old Capitol" in *Old Capitol Reconditioning Folder*, 1921–1922, p. 51. Includes some correspondence and reports, 1917–1923. University of Iowa Archives.

12 Walter Prichard Eaton, "A University on Main Street," *McNaught's Monthly*, October 1925, p. 117.

13 Jessup File, 1923–1924, Folder No. 52. Agreement between the contractor and the board of education's finance committee attached to letter from Fisk to Jessup dated January 25, 1924. University of Iowa Archives.

14 Jessup File, 1921–1922, Folder No. 5. Letter from John M. Fisk to George T. Baker, chairman of the board of education's Special Committee for Repairs and Fireproofing Old Capitol, December 2, 1922. University of Iowa Archives.

15 Smith, "Old Capitol Spiral Stairs," December 11, 1934, in "Old Capitol Reconstruction Album."

16 Interview, Walter Siechert, Cedar Rapids, Iowa, February 26, 1971.

17 Photograph in slide file, Old Capitol office.

18 See note 16.

19 Minard Lafever, *The Beauties of Modern Architecture* (New York: D. Appleton and Co., 1835), Plate 43.

20 Betsy H. Woodman, "John Francis Rague: Mid-Nineteenth Century Revivalist Architect (1799–1877)" (Master's thesis, University of Iowa, 1969), pp. 6–10.

21 "With Other Editors: The Old Capitol (from the *Des Moines Register*)," *Daily Iowan*, January 14, 1928, p. 4.

4. The Architectural Restoration, 1970–1976

1 Willard L. Boyd, "Old Capitol." Speech given at fund-raising dinners in 1972 and 1973 to finance the restoration of Old Capitol.

2 "UI's Old Capitol to be Restored as Historical Site," *Iowa City Press-Citizen*, Saturday, July 18, 1970, p. 1.

3 Records of the Board of Trustees, 1880, p. 169. University of Iowa Archives.

4 Smith, "Old Capitol Reconstruction Album."

5 *Journal of the House of Representatives of the Third Legislative Assembly of the Territory of Iowa* [1840], pp. 191–192.

6 *Iowa Capital Reporter*, December 13, 1854, p. 2.

7 *Journal of the House of Representatives of the State of Iowa* [1854] (Iowa City: D. A. Mahony and J. B. Dorr, Printers, 1855), p. 9.

8 *Iowa City Republican*, June 27, 1856, p. 2.

9 *Journal of the House of Representatives of the Sixth General Assembly of the State of Iowa* [1856] (Iowa City: P. Moriarty, Printer, 1857), p. 31.

10 Shambaugh, p. 105.

11 Noah Webster, *An American Dictionary of the English Language* (Springfield, Mass.: Published by George and Charles Merriam, 1853), p. 491.

12 "Reactions Favorable to Funding for Restoration of Old Capitol," *Iowa City Press-Citizen*, February 8, 1974, p. 4B.

5. The Interior

1 *Acts, Resolutions and Memorials Passed at the Regular Session of the Third General Assembly of the State of Iowa* [1850], p. 223.

2 *Journal of the House of Representatives of the Seventh Legislative Assembly of the Territory of Iowa* [1845] (Fort Madison: R. Wilson Albright, Printer, 1845), p. 209.

3 *Legislative and Contingent Expenses of the Territory of Iowa.* Account No. 80,345. National Archives, Washington, D.C., p. 47.

4 Thomas H. Ormsbee, *Field Guide to Early American Furniture* (New York: Bonanza Books, 1951), p. 87.

5 *Legislative and Contingent Expenses.* Account No. 77,099. National Archives, Washington, D.C., p. 20.

6 "Old Cap Workmen Realize Their Part in Iowa History," *Cedar Rapids Gazette*, September 7, 1975, p. 3B.

7 See note 6.

8 See note 6.

9 "Old Capitol: Restoration of a Landmark," film made by graduate students in the Department of Speech and Dramatic Art, University of Iowa, 1972–1977.

6. The Dedication

1 English translation of the benediction delivered at the dedication of Old Capitol, July 3, 1976, by Frank Wanatee, Sr. The complete program of the ceremony may be found in appendix C.

Select Bibliography

Primary Sources

Manuscripts

Ambrose, Fred. Box No. 5: Building Information A–O. University of Iowa
Archives.

Briggs, Ansel. Papers, State Historical Society of Iowa, Des Moines.

Cartwright, M. Etta. "Poweshiek's Oration and Reminiscences," n.d., State
Historical Society of Iowa, Iowa City.

Chambers, John. Papers, State Historical Society of Iowa, Des Moines.

Clarke, James. Papers, State Historical Society of Iowa, Des Moines.

College of Liberal Arts Faculty Minutes, 1860–1945, University of Iowa
Archives.

Council File No. 6, 1840, State Historical Society of Iowa, Des Moines.

Council File No. 63, 1841, State Historical Society of Iowa, Des Moines.

Fisk, John M. Faculty/Staff Folder, University of Iowa Archives.

Grimes, James W. Papers, State Historical Society of Iowa, Des Moines.

Grounds and Buildings Files. 1921–1922, 1922–1923, 1923–1924, 1924–1925,
exhibits of the Board of Regents and Finance Committee, University of
Iowa Archives.

Hempstead, Stephen. Papers, State Historical Society of Iowa, Des Moines.

Jessup, Walter A. Faculty/Staff Folders. 1921–1922, Folder No. 5, Grounds
and Buildings; 1922–1923, File No. 5, Grounds and Buildings; File No. 11,
Old Capitol Fireproofing; File No. 15, Miscellaneous; File No. 30, Secretary's Office; File No. 36, Correspondence and Miscellaneous; File No. 41,
Graphic and Plastic Arts; 1923–1924, File No. 52, Grounds and Buildings;
1924–1925, File No. 51, Grounds and Buildings; University of Iowa
Archives.

Law Needs Manuscript File. University of Iowa Archives.

Lucas, Robert. Papers, 1803–1906. Manuscript Collection, State Historical Society of Iowa, Iowa City.

Lucas, Robert. Papers, State Historical Society of Iowa, Des Moines.

Minutes of the Meetings of the State Board of Education and Finance Committee. July 1, 1920–June 30, 1921; July 1, 1921–June 30, 1922; July 1, 1922–June 30, 1923; July 1, 1923–June 30, 1924; July 1, 1924–June 30, 1925. University of Iowa Archives.

Old Capitol File. University of Iowa Archives.

Old Capitol, Father Mazzuchelli File. University of Iowa Archives.

Old Capitol Reconditioning File. University of Iowa Archives.

Olmsted Brothers. Report, April 10, 1905, University of Iowa Archives.

Proudfoot and Bird, Architects. Architectural blue-line prints of various university buildings [includes Old Capitol, 1912 and 1922], University of Iowa Archives.

Rague, John F. Letters, 1840 and 1856, State Historical Society of Iowa, Des Moines.

Records of the Board of Trustees [Board of Trustees, 1847–1870; Board of Regents, 1870–1909; State Board of Education, 1909–1955; Board of Regents, 1955–present], University of Iowa Archives.

Reno, Morgan. *Catalogue of the Iowa Territorial Library.* Iowa City, 1845.

"Report of the Special Committee of the State Board of Education," July 3, 1923. Included in "Old Capitol Reconstruction Album," Old Capitol, University of Iowa Archives, State Historical Society of Iowa, Iowa City.

Ronalds, John. Papers, State Historical Society of Iowa, Iowa City.

Sanders, Cyrus. "Journal, Johnson County, Iowa Territory," December 6, 1838–January 6, 1845, State Historical Society of Iowa, Iowa City.

Shambaugh, Benjamin Franklin. Faculty/Staff Folder, University of Iowa Archives.

Vouchers. Capitol at Iowa City, 1841, 1842, 1844, 1845, 1846, 1847, 1848, 1849, 1853, 1854, State Historical Society of Iowa, Des Moines.

Vouchers. Labor and Materials, Capitol Building, 1844–1857, State Historical Society of Iowa, Des Moines.

Vouchers. Capitol at Iowa City, Payrolls for 1841, 1842, 1843, 1844, 1847, State Historical Society of Iowa, Des Moines.

Vouchers, Miscellaneous. Capitol at Iowa City, 1845–1847, 1850–1852, State Historical Society of Iowa, Des Moines.

Vouchers, Miscellaneous. Capitol at Iowa City, 1839–1843, State Historical Society of Iowa, Des Moines.

Yewell, George H. Journals, University of Iowa Archives.

Government Documents

Acts and Joint Resolutions Passed at the Regular Session of the Thirty-Seventh General Assembly of the State of Iowa. Des Moines: State of Iowa, 1917.

Acts and Resolutions Passed at the First Session of the General Assembly of the State of Iowa [1846]. Iowa City: A. H. Palmer, Printer, 1847.

Acts and Resolutions Passed at the Regular Session of the Seventh General Assembly of the State of Iowa [1857]. Des Moines: J. Teesdale, State Printer, 1858.

Acts Passed at the First Session of the Legislative Assembly of the Territory of Wisconsin [1836]. Belmont, W.T.: James Clarke, Printer to the Legislative Assembly, 1836.

Acts, Resolutions and Memorials Passed at the Extra Session of the Fifth General Assembly of the State of Iowa [1856]. Iowa City: P. Moriarty, State Printer, 1856.

Acts, Resolutions and Memorials Passed at the Extra Session of the First General Assembly of the State of Iowa [1848]. Iowa City: A. H. Palmer, Printer, 1848.

Acts, Resolutions and Memorials Passed at the Regular Session of the Fifth General Assembly of the State of Iowa [1854]. Iowa City: D. A. Mahony & J. B. Dorr, State Printers, 1855.

Acts, Resolutions and Memorials Passed at the Regular Session of the Fourth General Assembly of the State of Iowa [1852]. Iowa City: Wm. H. Merritt, State Printer, 1853.

Acts, Resolutions and Memorials Passed at the Regular Session of the Second General Assembly of the State of Iowa [1848]. Iowa City: Printed by Palmer & Paul, 1849.

Acts, Resolutions and Memorials Passed at the Regular Session of the Sixth General Assembly of the State of Iowa [1856]. Iowa City: P. Moriarty, State Printer, 1857.

Acts, Resolutions and Memorials Passed at the Regular Session of the Third General Assembly of the State of Iowa [1850]. Iowa City: Palmer & Paul, State Printers, 1851.

Construction of Rooms in the Iowa State Capitol to Serve As Court Rooms for the U.S. District Court. Account No. 100,452, with Thomas Snyder. National Archives, Washington, D.C.

Construction of Rooms in the Iowa State Capitol to Serve As Court Rooms for the U.S. District Court. Account No. 101,575, with Doty and Lindsey Company. National Archives, Washington, D.C.

Construction of Rooms in the Iowa State Capitol to Serve As Court Rooms for the U.S. District Court. Account No. 102,567, with J. S. Handy. National Archives, Washington, D.C.

Construction of the Capitol Building in Iowa City. Account Nos. 79,180; 79,792. National Archives, Washington, D.C.

Contingent Expenses of the Governor of the Territory of Iowa. Account Nos. 77,498; 86,943; 89,959; 100,578. National Archives, Washington, D.C.

Contingent Expenses of the Territory of Iowa. Account Nos. 93,539; 94,488; 95,809; 95,953; 96,452; 97,377. National Archives, Washington, D.C.

Fourth (4th) Territory Assembly, 1841. Bills and Memorials; Claims and Communications. Six 22. State Historical Society of Iowa, Des Moines.

Journal of the Council of the Eighth Legislative Assembly of the Territory of Iowa [1845]. Dubuque: George Greene, Printer, 1846.

Journal of the Council of the Fifth Legislative Assembly of the Territory of Iowa [1842]. Davenport: Alfred Sander, Printer, 1843.

Journal of the Council of the First Legislative Assembly of the Territory of Iowa [1838]. Dubuque: Russell & Reeves, Printer, 1839.

Journal of the Council of the Fourth Legislative Assembly of the Territory of Iowa [1841]. Bloomington: Jno. B. Russell, Printer, 1842.

Journal of the Council of the Second Legislative Assembly of the Territory of Iowa [1839]. Burlington: James G. Edwards, Printer, 1840.

Journal of the Council of the Seventh Legislative Assembly of the Territory of Iowa [1844]. Iowa City: Williams & Palmer, Printers, 1845.

Journal of the Council of the Sixth Legislative Assembly of the Territory of Iowa [1843]. Burlington: James G. Edwards, Printer, 1844.

Journal of the Council of the Third Legislative Assembly of the Territory of Iowa [1840]. Bloomington: Russell & Hughes, Printers, 1841.

Journal of the House of Representatives of the State of Iowa, at the Special Session [1856]. Iowa City: P. Moriarty, State Printer, 1856.

Journal of the House of Representatives of the Eighth Legislative Assembly of the Territory of Iowa [1845]. Keosauqua: J. and J. M. Shepherd, Printers, 1846.

Journal of the House of Representatives of the Eleventh General Assembly of the State of Iowa. Des Moines: F. W. Palmer, State Printer, 1866.

Journal of the House of Representatives of the Fifth Legislative Assembly of the Territory of Iowa [1842]. Iowa City: William Crum, Printer, 1843.

Journal of the House of Representatives of the First Legislative Assembly of the Territory of Iowa [1838]. Burlington: Clarke & M'Kenny, Printers, 1839.

Journal of the House of Representatives of the Fourth Legislative Assembly of the Territory of Iowa [1841]. Dubuque: Wilson & Keesecker, Printers, 1842.

Journal of the House of Representatives of the General Assembly of the State of Iowa [1846]. Burlington: Printed at the Hawk-Eye Office, 1847.

Journal of the House of Representatives of the General Assembly of the State of Iowa [1850]. Iowa City: Palmer & Paul, State Printers, 1850.

Journal of the House of Representatives of the General Assembly of the State of

Iowa, at the Extra Session Thereof [1848]. Keosauqua: Des Moines Valley Whig Office, Printer, 1848.

Journal of the House of Representatives of the Second Legislative Assembly of the Territory of Iowa [1839]. Burlington: Printed by J. Gardner Edwards, 1840.

Journal of the House of Representatives of the Second Regular Session of the General Assembly of the State of Iowa [1848]. Fort Madison: Statesman Office, Printer, 1850.

Journal of the House of Representatives of the Seventh Legislative Assembly of the Territory of Iowa [1845]. Fort Madison: R. Wilson Albright, Printer, 1845.

Journal of the House of Representatives of the Sixth General Assembly of the State of Iowa [1856]. Iowa City: P. Moriarty, Printer, 1857.

Journal of the House of Representatives of the Sixth Legislative Assembly of the Territory of Iowa [1843]. Dubuque: Wilson and Keesecker, Printers, 1844.

Journal of the House of Representatives of the State of Iowa [1852]. Iowa City: Wm. H. Merritt, Printer, 1852.

Journal of the House of Representatives of the State of Iowa [1854]. Iowa City: D. A. Mahony and J. B. Dorr, Printers, 1855.

Journal of the House of Representatives of the Third Legislative Assembly of the Territory of Iowa [1840]. Dubuque: Wm. W. Coriell, Printer, 1841.

Journal of the House of Representatives of the United States. December 3, 1838. Washington: Printed by Thomas Allen, 1839.

Journals of the Second Legislative Assembly of the Territory of Iowa, Special Session [1840]. Dubuque: Telegraph Herald, July 13, 1902. [Reprint of Council and House of Representatives Sessions.]

Journal of the Senate at the Extra Session of the First General Assembly of the State of Iowa [1848]. Iowa City: Printer for A. H. Palmer by Palmer & Paul, 1848.

Journal of the Senate of the First General Assembly of the State of Iowa [1846]. Iowa City: A. H. Palmer, Printer, 1847.

Journal of the Senate of the Fourth General Assembly of the State of Iowa [1852]. Iowa City: Wm. H. Merritt, State Printer, 1853.

Journal of the Senate, at the Second Regular Session of the General Assembly of the State of Iowa [1848]. Andrew: Printed at the Jackson County Democrat Office, 1849.

Journal of the Senate of the Sixth General Assembly of the State of Iowa [1856]. Iowa City: P. Moriarty, State Printer, 1857.

Journal of the Senate of the State of Iowa [1854]. Iowa City: D. A. Mahony and J. B. Dorr, State Printers, 1855.

Journal of the Senate of the State of Iowa at the Special Session [July 1856]. Iowa City: P. Moriarty, State Printer, 1857.

Journal of the Senate of the Third General Assembly of the State of Iowa [1850]. Iowa City: Palmer & Paul, State Printers, 1850.

Laws of Iowa, Passed at the Extra Session of the Legislative Assembly [1844]. And *The Laws of the Regular Session* [1845]. Iowa City: Williams & Palmer, Printers, 1845.

Laws of Iowa, Passed at the Session of the Legislative Assembly [1843]. Burlington: James Clarke, Printer, 1844.

Laws of Iowa, Seventh General Assembly [1858]. Des Moines: J. Teesdale, State Printer, 1858.

Laws of the Fifth General Assembly [1855]. Iowa City: P. Moriarty, Printer, 1856.

Laws of the First General Assembly [1846–1847]. Published by Authority. Iowa City: A. H. Palmer, Printer, 1847.

Laws of the Fortieth General Assembly [1923]. Des Moines: The State of Iowa, 1923.

Laws of the Territory of Iowa [1839]. Burlington: J. H. M'Kenny, Printer, 1840.

Laws of the Territory of Iowa, Passed at the Extra Session of the Legislative Assembly [1840]. Burlington: M. H. M'Kenny, Printer, 1840.

Laws of the Twelfth General Assembly [1868]. Des Moines: F. W. Palmer, State Printer, 1868.

Laws of the Thirty-Seventh General Assembly [1917]. Des Moines: State of Iowa, 1917.

Legislative and Contingent Expenses of the Territory of Iowa. Account Nos. 77,099; 80,251; 80,345; 81,586; 84,927; 89,070; 94,750. National Archives, Washington, D.C.

Legislative Expenses of the Territory of Iowa. Account Nos. 81,355; 81,769; 90,264; 92,037; 93,164. National Archives, Washington, D.C.

Purchase of a Library for the Territorial Government of the Territory of Iowa. Account No. 86,053. National Archives, Washington, D.C.

Purchase of Stove and Utensils for Governor's Office of the Territory of Iowa. Account No. 87,149. National Archives, Washington, D.C.

Report of the Joint Committee Appointed to Visit the State University and Deaf and Dumb Asylum. 1866.

The Code of Iowa, Passed at the Session of the General Assembly of 1850–1851, and Approved 5th February, 1851. Iowa City: Palmer & Paul, State Printers, 1851.

The Statute Laws of the Territory of Iowa [1838–39]. Dubuque: Russell & Reeves, Printers, 1839.

United States Treasury Department. *Letters from Executives of Territories.* December 12, 1838–December 2, 1856. National Archives, Washington, D.C.

Maps

Map of Iowa City. Drawn by L. [Leander] Judson, July 4, 1839, Plat
Record 1, p. 116, Recorder's Office, Johnson County, Iowa [Retraced by
S. S. Hovey, May 12, 1906].
Map of Iowa City, Johnson County, Iowa, and Its Environs. Compiled and
drawn by J. H. Millar, Bryan & Millar, Panora, Iowa. Illustrations by
G. [George] H. Yewel [*sic*]. Lithographed by W. Schuchman, Pittsburgh,
Pennsylvania, 1854.
Sanborn Map Company. *Iowa City, Iowa,* June 1899, p. 12. State Historical
Society of Iowa, Iowa City.

Photographs

Calvin, Samuel. Collecton of Negative Contact Images. Department of Ge-
ology, University of Iowa.
Crumley Photo Albums. Manuscript Division, State Historical Society of
Iowa, Iowa City.
Old Capitol Photograph File. University of Iowa Archives.
"Old Capitol Reconstruction Album." Compiled by A. A. Smith, Superin-
tendent of Buildings and Grounds, University of Iowa. Circa 1934. Photo-
graphs and reports. Old Capitol, University of Iowa Archives, State His-
torical Society of Iowa, Iowa City.
Wetherby, Isaac. Collection. Glass plate negatives, daguerreotypes, photo-
graphs, papers, and caricatures from 1850–1870. Putnam Museum,
Davenport.

Newspapers

Ballou's (Gleason's) Pictorial Drawing Room Companion. As Gleasons, Vol.
1–5, 1851–1854; as Ballou's, Vol. 9–12, 14, 16–17, 1855–1859.
Bloomington Herald, Bloomington [Muscatine], 1840–1849.
Burlington Hawk-Eye and Iowa Patriot, Burlington, 1839–1843.
Cedar Rapids Gazette, Cedar Rapids, 1975.
Daily Iowan, University of Iowa, Iowa City, 1901–1928; 1945–1970.
Daily Republican, Iowa City, 1876–1902.
Des Moines Register, Des Moines, 1916–1930; 1970–1976.
Dubuque Visitor, Dubuque, 1836–1837.
Iowa Capital Reporter, Iowa City, 1841–1855.
Iowa City Herald, Iowa City, 1894–1897.
Iowa City Press-Citizen, Iowa City, 1920–1930; 1970–1988.
Iowa City Republican, 1856–1857; 1862–1901.
Iowa City Weekly Republican, Iowa City, 1858–1859.

Iowa News, Dubuque, 1837–1839.
Iowa Patriot, Burlington, 1839.
Iowa Standard, Iowa City, 1842–1848.
Iowa State Press, Iowa City, 1871–1904.
Iowa Statesman, Fort Madison, 1850–1851.
Iowa Sun, Davenport, 1839–1842.
Iowa Territorial Gazette and Burlington Advertiser, Burlington, 1838–1840.
Sangamo Journal, Springfield, Illinois, 1840.
Tri-Weekly Muscatine Journal, Muscatine, 1854–1858.
University Reporter, University of Iowa, Iowa City, 1868–1881.
Vidette, University of Iowa, Iowa City, 1879–1881.
Vidette-Reporter, University of Iowa, Iowa City, 1881–1900.

Books

A Glimpse of Iowa in 1846: or the Emigrant's Guide. Burlington: W. D. Skillman, Publisher, 1846.
Benton, Thomas H. Jr. *History of the University of Iowa 1840–1867*. Davenport: Gazette Company, Printer, 1877.
The Journal of Design and Manufactures. London: Chapman and Hall. Volumes 1–6, March 1849–February 1852.
Lafever, Minard. *The Beauties of Modern Architecture*. New York: D. Appleton and Co., 1835.
Mazzuchelli, Samuel Charles. Reprint. *The Memoirs of Father Samuel Mazzuchelli, O.P.* Chicago: Priory Press, 1967.
Newhall, J. B. *A Glimpse of Iowa in 1846*. [Reprint by State Historical Society of Iowa, Iowa City in 1957.] Burlington, Iowa: W. D. Skillman, Publisher, 1846.
Parker, Nathan H. *The Iowa Handbook, for 1856*. Boston: John P. Jewett and Company, 1856.
Stuart, James, and Revett, Nicholas. *The Antiquities of Athens*. London: Henry G. Bohn, 1858.
Webster, Noah. *An American Dictionary of the English Language*. Springfield, Mass.: Published by George and Charles Merriam, 1853.
Webster, Thomas, and Parks, Frances. *An Encyclopedia of Domestic Economy*. New York: Harper and Brothers, 1849.
Well's Pocket Hand-Book of IOWA: Past, Present, and Prospective. New York: John G. Wells Publishing Agent, 1857.

Periodicals

Circulars, Catalogues, Reports, Etc., of the State University of Iowa. From September 1, 1855–1860, inclusive. Reprint. Davenport: Gazette Company, 1877.

The Hawkeye, 1893, 1894, 1905, 1906. Old Capitol, University of Iowa Archives.

Iowa Alumnus, 1903–1922. University of Iowa Archives.

McClain, Emlin. "Law Department of the State University of Iowa," *The Green Bag*, September 1889, pp. 374–394.

University of Iowa Catalogues. 1856–1862, 1861–1862 to 1976–1978. Old Capitol, University of Iowa Archives.

Secondary Sources

Manuscripts

Boyd, Willard L. "Old Capitol," speech given at fund-raising dinners for the restoration of Old Capitol, 1972–1973, Willard L. Boyd speech file, President's Office, Old Capitol. Also at University of Iowa Archives.

———. "Remarks on the Occasion of the Rededication of Old Capitol," Iowa City, Iowa, July 2, 1976, President's Office, Old Capitol.

"Building Register for the University of Iowa," University Business Office, University of Iowa.

Gray, Steve. "Proudfoot and Bird." Paper, Iowa State University, 1975, University of Iowa Archives.

"Legislation Relating to the State University of Iowa, Part I and Part II," compiled at University of Iowa Archives.

"Old Capitol History, 1970–," as reported in published sources. Susan C. Hancher, comp. Old Capitol Office.

Plank, E. A. to Virgil M. Hancher. Letter, June 27, 1955. Virgil M. Hancher Correspondence File, 1955, University of Iowa Archives.

Rossman, Kenneth. "History of the College of Law of the University of Iowa: 1885–1920." Paper, n.d., University of Iowa Archives.

Shambaugh Collection. Documentary Material. University of Iowa Archives.

Shambaugh Family Papers. Benjamin Franklin Shambaugh Series. Box 1, Manuscripts. Folders 17–19. "History of Iowa City." Box 2. Folder 11. Old Capitol, Iowa City, notes regarding building of Old Capitol from personal recollections of Geo. H. Yewell recorded by Oscar C. Coast, December 26, 1922. Folders 12–14. The old stone capitol—data, et al. University of Iowa Archives.

Shambaugh Family Papers. Bertha Maude Horack Shambaugh Series. Boxes 19–31. House Books 1–20. Boxes 31–33. Ringfolds 1–9. University of Iowa Archives.

Sizemore, Jean Wolfe. "The Planning of the Pentacrest." Paper, University of Iowa, November 27, 1979, Old Capitol file, Old Capitol.

Books

A Century of Carpet and Rug Making in America. New York: Bigelow—
Hartford Carpet Co., 1925.

Alderson, Jo Bartels, and Alderson, J. Michael. *The Man Mazzuchelli, Pioneer Priest*. Madison, Wis.: Wisconsin House, Ltd., 1974.

Aurner, Charles [Clarence] Ray. *Leading Events in Johnson County, Iowa,
History*. Vol. 1: Historical, 1912; Vol. 12: Biographical, 1913. Cedar Rapids,
Iowa: Western Historical Press.

Bendure, Zelma. *America's Fabrics: Origin, History, Manufacture, Characteristics and Uses*. New York: Macmillan Co., 1946.

Birrel, Verla. *The Textile Arts*. New York: Harper and Row, 1959.

Birren, Faber. *Color for Interiors: Historical and Modern*. New York:
Whitney Library of Design, n.d.

Boger, Louise Ade, and Boger, H. Patterson. *The Dictionary of Antiques and
the Decorative Arts*. New York: Charles Scribner's Sons, 1957.

Boger, Louise Ade. *The Complete Guide to Furniture Styles*. New York:
Charles Scribner's Sons, 1969.

Britten, F. J. *Old Clocks and Watches and Their Makers*. New York: Bonanza
Books, 1956.

Butler, Joseph T. *American Antiques 1800–1900*. New York: Odyssey Press,
1965.

Cole, Arthur H., and Williamson, Harold F. *The American Carpet Manufacture*. Cambridge: Harvard University Press, 1941.

Comstock, Helen, ed. *The Concise Encyclopedia of American Antiques*. Vols. I
and II. New York: Hawthorn Books, Inc., Publishers, 1958.

Crockett, Norman L. *The Woolen Industry of the Midwest*. Lexington: University Press of Kentucky, 1970.

Depew, Chauncey M. *100 Years of American Commerce*. New York: D. O.
Haynes and Co., 1895.

Gowans, Alan. *Images of American Living*. Philadelphia and New York: J. B.
Lippincott Co., 1964.

Gue, Benjamin F. *Biographies and Portraits of the Progressive Men of Iowa
and History of the State*. Des Moines: Conaway & Shaw, 1899.

———. *History of Iowa*. Vols. I–IV. New York: Century History Company,
1903.

Hamlin, Talbot. *Greek Revival Architecture in America*. New York: Oxford
University Press, 1944.

History of Johnson County, Iowa from 1836 to 1882. Iowa City, Iowa: no publisher given, 1883.

Hitchcock, Henry-Russell. *Architecture: Nineteenth and Twentieth Centuries*.
Baltimore: Penguin Books, 1963.

————, and Seale, William. *Temples of Democracy: The State Capitols of the U.S.A.* New York: Harcourt Brace Jovanovich, 1976.

Kauffman, Henry J. *The American Fireplace.* Nashville: Thomas Nelson, Inc., 1972.

Miller, Mary H., comp. *Historical Sketch of the Iowa State Library.* Des Moines, 1893.

Morrison, Hugh. *Early American Architecture.* New York: Oxford University Press, 1952.

National Park Service. *Historic American Building Survey.* Washington, D.C.: Government Printing Office, 1941.

Old Settlers' Association Yearbooks, Johnson County, Iowa, 1866–1925. [Reports of Annual Reunions; no publisher given.]

Ormsbee, Thomas H. *Field Guide to Early American Furniture.* New York: Bonanza Books, 1951.

————. *Field Guide to American Victorian Furniture.* New York: Bonanza Books, 1952.

Petersen, William J. *The Story of Iowa.* Vols. I–IV. New York: Lewis Historical Publishing Company, Inc., 1952.

Shambaugh, Benjamin F., ed. *Documentary Material Relating to the History of Iowa.* Vols. I–III. Iowa City: State Historical Society of Iowa, 1897.

————, ed. *Executive Journal of Iowa, 1838–1841, of Governor Robert Lucas.* Iowa City: State Historical Society of Iowa, 1906.

————. *Iowa City, A Contribution to the Early History of Iowa.* Iowa City: State Historical Society of Iowa, 1893.

————. *The Old Stone Capitol Remembers.* Iowa City: State Historical Society of Iowa, 1939.

Winchester, Alice. *How to Know American Antiques.* New York: New American Library of World Literature, 1951.

Periodicals

Aumann, F. R. "Poweshiek." *The Palimpsest,* September 1927, pp. 297–305.

Aurner, Clarence Ray. "The Story of the Old Capitol." *Iowa Alumnus,* October 1921, pp. 12–14.

Born, W. "Cotton Prints of the 18th and 19th Centuries." *CIBA Review,* October 1949, p. 76.

Brandt, Isaac. "Removal of State Capital to Des Moines." Eighth Reunion of the *Pioneer Lawmakers' Association of Iowa.* Des Moines: Bernard Murphy, State Printer, 1902.

Briggs, John Ely. "The Removal of the Capital from Iowa City to Des Moines." *Iowa Journal of History and Politics,* 1916, pp. 456–495.

Brigham, Johnson. "Pioneer History of the Territorial and State Library of Iowa." *Annals of Iowa*, October 1912, pp. 481–538; January 1913, pp. 590–628.

"Carpet Weaving." *Antiques*, June 1935, p. 240.

Craig, James. "The 1840 North Carolina Capitol and Its Furniture." *Antiques*, August 1965, pp. 205–207.

Dye, Eva Emery. "The Historic Capitol of Iowa." *Magazine of American History*, June 1889, pp. 443–455.

Eaton, Walter P. "A University on Main Street." *McNaught's Monthly*, October 1925, pp. 117–118.

Everett, Ethel Walton. "Ingrain Carpets." *Hobbies*, February 1953, pp. 108–109.

Hansen, Millard W. "The Early History of the College of Law, State University of Iowa: 1865–1884." *Iowa Law Review*, November 1944, pp. 31–67.

Henderson, Earl W., Jr. "Sleuthing the Mid-1900s." *AIA Journal*, November 1967; reprinted, n.p.

Hoffman, M. M. "John Francis Rague: Pioneer Architect of Iowa." *Annals of Iowa*, 1934, pp. 444–448.

Irish, F. M. "History of Johnson County, Iowa." *Annals of Iowa*, January 1868, pp. 23–31; April 1868, pp. 105–120; July 1868, pp. 191–215; October 1868, pp. 302–328.

Keyes, Margaret N. "A Home Economist Does Historic Preservation." *Journal of Home Economics*, May 1975, pp. 19–22.

———. "Documentation for Restoration." *Proceedings of 1973 Annual Meeting and Preservation Conference*, National Trust for Historic Preservation, Washington, D.C., 1974, pp. 18–19.

———. "In Search of an Original: The Restoration of Old Capitol." *The Iowan*, Fall 1977, pp. 5–13.

———. "Old Capitol: A Greek Revival Monument in Iowa." *The Victorian Society in America Newsletter*, Fall 1973, pp. 6–9.

———. "Old Capitol, Iowa City, Iowa." *The Magazine Antiques*, July 1978, pp. 120–131. Reprinted in *The Antiques Book of Victorian Interiors*, Elizabeth D. Garrett, comp., 1981.

———. "Old Capitol Restored." *The Palimpsest*, July–August 1976, pp. 122–128.

———. "Piecing Together Iowa's Old Capitol." *Historic Preservation*, January–March 1974, pp. 40–43.

———. "The Gallery Will Be Reserved for Ladies." *Annals of Iowa*, Summer 1973, pp. 1–16.

Lamb, Martha J. "The Historic Capitol of Iowa." *Magazine of American History*, June 1889, pp. 443–445.

Lathrop, Henry. "The Capitol and Capitals of Iowa." *Iowa Historical Record*, July 1888, pp. 97–124.

Mahan, Bruce E. "The Old Capitol Restored." In *Year Book of the Old Settlers' Association, Johnson County, Iowa, 1923–1924*, pp. 3–10.
———. "University of Iowa." *The Palimpsest*, February 1971, pp. 33–128.
Negus, Charles. "The Early History of Iowa." *Annals of Iowa*, October 1869, p. 326; January 1874, p. 13.
Plum, H. G. "The Old Stone Building." *Iowa Historical Record*, January 1896, pp. 418–425.
"Pounce Boxes and Sand Shakers." *Antiques*, July 1947, pp. 36–37.
Smith, C. Ray. "Restored National Monument Sparks Urban Revitalization." *Progressive Architecture*, February 1970, pp. 52–63.
"Use of Old Capitol in the 1860's." *Iowa Alumnus*, May 1912, p. 227.
Vincent, John R. "Early Lighting Devices in Iowa." *Annals of Iowa*, Winter 1964, pp. 195–205.
Wanerus, Theodore. "The Old Capitol Building: A Plea for its Preservation." *Iowa Alumnus*, February 1916, pp. 7–9.
Wright, Luella M. "Iowa's Oldest Library." *Iowa Journal of History and Politics*, 1940, pp. 409–428.

Theses

Baker, Ann M. "The Historic Textiles of Iowa's Old Capitol." Master's thesis, University of Iowa, 1974.
Bates, Katherine V. "History of the State University of Iowa: Aspects of the Physical Structure." Master's thesis, University of Iowa, 1949.
Carstensen, Vernon. "The State University of Iowa: The Collegiate Department from the Beginning to 1878." Ph.D. dissertation, University of Iowa, 1936.
Dawson, Steven Kent. "The Interior Design of the House of Representatives Chamber of Iowa's Old Capitol 1842–1857." Master's thesis, University of Iowa, 1972.
Fogdall, Vergil S. "History of the State University of Iowa." Ph.D. dissertation, University of Iowa, 1947.
Woodman, Betsy H. "John Francis Rague: Mid-Nineteenth Century Revivalist Architect (1799–1877)." Master's thesis, University of Iowa, 1969.

Interviews

Anderson, Lowell. Historical Sites Curator, Illinois State Historical Society, Springfield. February 1971.
Bentz, Dale M. Director, University Libraries, University of Iowa, Iowa City. July 1975.
Bloom, John Porter. Editor, *Territorial Papers of the United States*, National Archives, Washington, D.C. April 1971.

Dennis, Stephen N. Research Assistant, Institute of Government, University of North Carolina, Chapel Hill. July 1971.

Dunlap, Leslie W. Dean, University of Iowa Libraries, University of Iowa, Iowa City. December 1970.

Ellington, John. Director, Department of Art, Culture, and History, North Carolina Historical Society, Raleigh. July 1971.

Franklin, W. Neil. Territorial Papers Staff, National Archives, Washington, D.C. April 1971.

Greene, Lida L. Librarian, Iowa State Department of History and Archives, Des Moines. October 1970.

Harstad, Peter. Director, State Historical Society of Iowa, Iowa City. June 1974.

Hickey, James. Curator, Abraham Lincoln Collection, Illinois State Historical Society, Springfield. February 1971.

Hovey, Alma. Emeritus Professor of English, University of Iowa, Iowa City. August 1970.

Lyons, Clarence F. Archivist; Legislative, Judicial, and Diplomatic Records Division; National Archives; Washington, D.C. April 1971.

Musgrove, Jack. Curator, Iowa Department of History and Archives, Des Moines. October 1970.

Sanders, John. Director, Institute of Government, University of North Carolina, Chapel Hill. July 1971.

Schwengel, Fred. U.S. Representative, First Congressional District of Iowa, Davenport. January 1971.

Siechert, Walter. Carpenter during rehabilitation of 1920s, Cedar Rapids, Iowa. February 1971.

Index

Illustrations are indicated by **boldfaced** numbers.

Agassiz, Louis, 43
Alexander, Robert L., 120
Allds, Mrs. A. C., 19
American College Testing Program, 41
Amundsen, Roald, 43
Anderson, Lowell, 78–80

Baker, Ann M., 100, 103, 104, 120
Banbury, Thomas M., 18
Beall, Paul R., 103–104, 105, 106
Bezanson, Larayne, 88
Bezanson, Peter, 88
Boblitz, Jacob, 19
Bowen, Howard R., 45, 73, 74, 132
Boyd, Susan Kuehn, 37, 74, 117
Boyd, Willard L., xiii, 37, 73, 75, 86, 98, 117, 118, 119, 122, 137–38
Branstad, Terry E., 135
Brender, Harold, 115–16
Briggs, Ansel, 21
Burge, Adelaide L., 60
Burrell, Howard A., **38**
Bush, Dave, **92**
Butler, Walter, 12
Byington, O. A., 46, 47

Calvin, Samuel, 30, 34
Cantacuzene, Julia, 43
Carver, Lucille, 86, 88
Carver, Roy, 86, 88
Casady, Phineas M., 6, 7
Chambers, John, 11, 59
Civil War, 40
Clarke, James, 14, 21
Colman, John M., 13
Conklin, Dwight (family), 112
Culver, John, 135
Cumming, C. A., 58
Current, Anne, 112–13

Daughters of the American Revolution, 131
Dawson, Steven K., 81, 83, 120
Dean, Amos, 23, 24, 99, 100
Deere Foundation, 88
Dodge, A. C., 20
Downey, Hugh D., 24
Drinkwater, John, 43
Dubuque County Jail, 58
Dykstra, Robert D., 120

Elias, Tasim Olawale, 136

Ensign, Forrest, 31
Esbin, Martha, 111
Estes, Simon, 121
Evans, Evan, 19, 105

Fales, Joseph T., 14
Felkner, Henry, 17
Ferry and Henderson (architectural firm), 90
Finkbine and Lovelace (contracting firm), 23
Fisk, J. M., 57, 62
Foster, M. A., 17
Freedom, James O., 132
Frye, Northrop, 135

Garrett, Wendell, 135
Gaymon, Charles, 19, 96
Glaser, Lewis, 111–12
Grassley, Charles, 136
Grimes, James W., 21, 81
Grinnell, Josiah B., 105
Grinnell, Mary Lou, 110
Grinnell, Peter S., 110
Grinnell College, 105, 106

Haddock, William J., 31, **38**, 39
Hall Foundation, 88
Hampton, Mrs. A. F., 19
Hanby and Heron (lumber company), 17
Hancher, Susan, xiii, 74, 110, 113, 118, 137
Hart, Anson, 13, 18, 96
Hempstead, Stephen, 21
Henderson, Earl W., Jr., 90
Herrick Historical Fund, 132
Hitchcock, Henry-Russell, 118
Holt, Mrs., 19
Hoover, Herbert, 43
Hopkins, Paul, 133
Houghton, Clark, 118
Hoxie, Vinnie Ream, 119

Illinois capitol (Springfield), 5, 6, **8**, 9, 52, 74, 76, 78–80, 90, 96, 97, 100, 103, 106, 107, 115
Iowa American Revolution Bicentennial Association, 88
Iowa City, 1–2, **3**, 15, **17**
Iowa City Antique Dealers' Association, 130
Iowa Heritage Roll of Honor, 89
Iowa High School Forensic League, 134
Iowa Law School (Des Moines), 28

Jensen, Viggo M. (contracting firm), 90
Jessup, Walter A., 40, 57, 58, 69, 71, 98
Johnson, Sylvanus, 17

Kennedy, John F., 41, 42
Kent, Fred W., 148
Kirkwood, Samuel J., 119
Kirkwood Community College, 119

Lafever, Minard, 67
Lennon, John, 136
Leonard, N. R., 25
Lincoln, Abraham, 40, 41, 42, 78
Lucas, Robert, 25, 59, 121, 135
Ludwig, Emil, 43

McColm, John and Thelma, 131
McDonald, William, 5
McGovern, George, 43
MacMillan, Donald, 43
Mason, Charles, 21
Mazzuchelli, Samuel Charles, 5–6, 9
Meyer, Joseph W., xiii
Michener, James A., 134
Miller, Franklin, 133
Morris, M. L., 16
Munro, Mr., 24

National Park Service, 87
National Register of Historic Places, 86–87, 135
National Trust for Historic Preservation, 133
North Carolina capitol (Raleigh), 80, 96, 97, 100, 103, 106, 107
Nye, Frank T., xiii

Old Capitol. *See also* University of Iowa
  administrative offices, 37, 69, 117, 119
  architect, 4–9. *See also* Rague, John Francis
  auditor's office, 25, 30, 31, 85, 110, **125**
  basement, 14, 24, 60, 77
  beams, 53–54, **53**, 89, 93, 107
  bell, 26, 118, 133–34
  board room. *See* University of Iowa, board room
  building materials, 2, 11–12, 17; limestone, 5–6, 9, 11, 12; quarries, 5, 8, 11, 12
  carpets. *See* floor coverings
  ceilings, 57, 93
  chimneys, 13, 69, 84, 85
  columns, 13, 146; Corinthian, 18, 52–53, 65, 67, **67, 68,** 118; Doric, 15, 17–18, **18,** 31, 53, 56, 65, 67
  construction, 9–18, 107
  cornerstone, 9, 20, 59, 76–77
  cornices, 56–57, 87
  cupola, 4, 5, 12–13, 14, 15, 18, 26, 52–53, 67, 89, 107, 118
  curtains. *See* window treatments
  descriptions, early, 2, 9, 11, 15, 77
  design styles. *See* period styles
  dome, 53
  draperies. *See* window treatments
  entrance, east, 56, **59,** 107

facade, east, **frontispiece, 29, 34**
facade, west, **55**
facelift (1981–82), 132
fences, 29
fireplaces, 19, 27, 69, 83–84, **84,** 113–14
fireproofing, 46–47, 48, 52, 57, 89
flag, 132
floor coverings, 19, 38, 71, 82, **104,** 109–110, 130, 131
floors, 17, 57, 59–60, 91, 92, 93, 130
foundation, 9, 48, 51–52, 56
frescoes, 24, 36, **37,** 56
funding, 9, 11, 12, 13, 14, 15, 16, 47, 48, 86–89, 132
furniture, 14, 18–20, 23, 24, 35–39, 69–70, 74, 94–109, **98, 99, 104, 108,** 111–12, 116–17, 130–31
gifts, 88–89, 131
governor's office, 25, 31, 37, **38,** 84, 86, 88, 97, 110, 114, **124,** 130, 131
ground floor. *See* basement
gutters, 52
hall, **127, 128**
heating. *See* fireplaces; stoves
historic events, 20–21, 39–45, 117–18, 121–23, **123,** 133–36
House chamber, 22, 26, 28, 31, 36, **36, 49,** 57, 63, 69, 71, 77, 81, 85, **85,** 86, 87, 89, 90, **92,** 97, **104,** 109, 110, 112, 114, 115, 116, **129;** furnishings, 97–106, 109, 116–17; gallery, 15, 81–83, **83, 92.** *See also* staircases
improvements (1866), 27–28
inscriptions, 58–59, **59**
landscaping, 15, 56, 132
library, territorial-state, 12, 14, 25, 77, 86, 88, 97, 106, 110, 111, 113, **113,** 114, **126,** 130, 131. *See also* University of Iowa, library

Old Capitol (*continued*)
lighting, 19–20, 29, 36, **70,** 71, 90,
114–15, 131
lintels, 54, **54,** 86
locks and keys, 106, **107**
millwork, 57, 58, 91
modillions, 56–57
names for (variants), xiii, 29, 32,
National Historic Landmark, 121
outbuildings, 28. *See also* University of Iowa, water closet period styles: American Empire, 95; Early Victorian, 95; Egyptian Revival, 58; Empire, 58; Georgian, 58; Gothic Revival, 95, 113; Greek Classical Revival, 5, 58, 110; Late Federal, 95; Renaissance Revival, 38; Rococo Revival, 95
plans, 2, 4–5, 6, 9, **10,** 11, 12–13, 14–15, 16, 46, 53, 54, 67, 76–77, 78, 94, 147
porch, 15, 54
porticos, 12, 77; east, 15–16, 56, 67, 136; west, 48, 54, 56
president's office. *See* University of Iowa, president's office
publications, 137
rehabilitation (1921–24), 13, 46–72, **50, 51, 53,** 91; expenses, 47, 48, 53, 58; exterior, 48–56, 67, 69; furnishings, 69–70; interior, 56–67; legislation, 47–48
remodeling (1857), 22–23
renovation. *See* rehabilitation
restoration (1970–76), 73–93; architectural, 73–93; committee offices, 117, 119; dedication, 118, 121–23, **123,** 143–44; expenses, 86, 87, 90; funding, 86–89, 132; interior, 94–120; research, 75–86, **79,** 95–97; student involvement, 75, 81, 112–13, 120,

142; workers, 115–17. *See also* Old Capitol Restoration Committee
roof, 12, 16, 27–28, 52, 89
rugs. *See* floor coverings
secretary of state's office, 12, 22, 77
Senate chamber, 23, 24, 30, 31, 32, 38, **39,** 57, 69, **70,** 71, 73, 74, 77, 83, **128,** 133, 134, 135, 137
settling (repairs), 48, **49, 50,** 51, **51,** 60
shutters. *See* window treatments
souvenirs, 54
staircases: basement (ground floor), 24, 60, **61,** 63; House chamber gallery, 91, **92,** 116; spiral, 15, 18, 51, 54, 60–65, **61, 64, 65, 66,** 90–91, 107, 115, **127**
stoves, 19, 27, 83–85, 113–14
Supreme Court chamber, 14, 24, 25, 31, 39, **54,** 74, 77, 84, **84,** 86, 88, 97, 109, 110, 114, 115, **126,** 131, 134
terrace, west, 44, **44,** 56, **57,** 132
tours, 137
treasurer's office, 85, 110, 114, **125,** 131
volunteer program, 137
walls: exterior, 51–52, 67, 69, 89, 90; interior, 17, 38, 56–57, 58, 83, 90, 91. *See also* frescoes
water closet, 28. *See also* University of Iowa, water closet
window treatments, 12–13, 19, 36, 37, 71, 85, 91, 97, 131
Old Capitol Endowment Fund, 131
Old Capitol Restoration Committee, xiii–xiv, 74–75, 76, 89, 94, 95, 133, 139–41
Old Capitol Schoolchildren's Program, 87–88
Old Settlers' Association, 94

Olmsted Brothers (landscaping firm), 35
Open Spaces Program for Historic Preservation, 87
Ormsbee, Thomas H., 100

Parden, Mary, 118
Parvin, Theodore S., 25
Pattee, William, 15, 16
Patton, W. H., 19
Phelan, Mary Kay, 87
Poweshiek, Chief, 1, 2, 122
Proudfoot, Bird and Rawson (architectural firm), 46, 56

quarries, 8, 11–12

Rague, John Francis, 4, 5, 6–9, **7**, 11, 13, 16, 52, 54, 58, 67, **68**, 77, 78, 90, 135
Ralston, Robert, 2
Ray, Robert D., 86, 89, 121, 122, 135
Redeker, Stanley, 86
Reno, Morgan, 14
Richardson, D. N., **38**
Rienow, Robert E., 60
Roberts, Peter, 19
Rockefeller, Nelson, 43
Ronalds, John, 2, 17
Royal Lichtenstein Circus, 136
Ruggles, C., 19
Ruppert, Charles, 116
Russell, George W. [pseud. AE], 43

Sadat, Anwar, 136
Schanz, Norman (furniture company), 103, **104**, 105, 106, 109, 116–17
Seale, William, 118–19
Shalla, Jim, **92**, 116
Shambaugh, Benjamin F., 5, 35, 37, 41, 43, 82
Siechert, Walter, 63, 65

Simmons, Eleanor Pownall, 88
Skeen, William, 5
Smith, A. A., 48, 54, 56, 57, 60, 62, 67, 77, 147
Smith, Dexter Edson, 23
Smith, Mike, 135
Smothers, Ann, 137
Snyder, Thomas, 19
Snyder, William B., 11, 12–13
Spencer, Oliver M., 25
Spriestersbach, D. C., 118, 119
Stanley, C. M., 86
State Historical Society of Iowa, 23–24, 25, 41, 80, 106, 134
Stefansson, Vilhjalmur, 43
Swalm, Albert W., **38**
Swan, Chauncey, 2, 4, 5, 9, 11, 21, 59, 77, 135
Sydell, Michael, 17, 146

Taft, Lorado, 41
Thomas, Norman, 43
Thompson, Bette, 119, 136, 137
Tillotson, Henry, 18
Tillotson, R. R., 18
Totten, Silas, 25, 69
Tyler, John, 59

United States Bicentennial, xiv, 78, 118, 123, 133
United States Department of Housing and Urban Development, 87
United States Department of the Interior, 87
United States Navy Pre-Flight unit, 40
University of Iowa
  administrative offices, 31, 47, 73–74, 75, 117, 148
  Alumni Association, 86
  Alumni Bureau of Information, 31
  Ancient and Modern Languages, Department of, 22

University of Iowa (*continued*)
Arab Student Association, 136
Armory, 30
athletics, 43
Board of Education, 46
board of regents, 37, **38**, 39, 40,
74, 86, 90, 91
board of trustees, 22, 24
board room, 71, 73, 74, 83; early,
31, 37, 38, **38**
Calvin Hall, **33**. *See also* Science
Hall
chapel: North Hall, 26, 27, 30;
Old Capitol, 22–23, 24, 27, 39
Collegiate Building, 32, **33**, 34
convocation, annual, 136
corn monument, 136
Dental Building, 32, **33**
Engineering, College of, 136
Erodelphian Society, 25
expansion, 26–35
Faculty Senate, 45, 134
fence, 29
finance committee, 31
fires, 32, 46–47
"Five Spot." *See* Pentacrest
Geology, Department of, 34
Graduate College, 117, 119
graduation ceremonies, 45
gymnasium, 30–31, 45
Hesperian Society, 25
Home Economics, Department of,
75, 110, 112
Induction Day, 45
Irving Institute, 25
janitor, 25–26, 31
Jessup Hall, 34, 56, 75
landscaping, 28, 35
Law, College of, 28, 30, 31, 32,
34, 35, **36**, 37, 45, 85, **85**
Law Building, 34
Law library, 28, 30, 32, 34, 35,
38–39, **39**

Liberal Arts, College of, 31, 45,
134
Liberal Arts, Hall of, 32
Library: North Hall, 30, **33**; Old
Capitol (Senate chamber), 23,
24, 30
literary societies, 25, 26, 40
Macbride Hall, 34
MacLean Hall, 34, 56
Mathematics and Natural Philoso-
phy, Department of, 22
Mechanics Academy, 22, 24
Medical Building, 32, **33**
Model School, 22, 24
Natural History Cabinet, 23, 27,
30
Natural Science, Department of,
30
Natural Science Building, 34
Normal Department, 22, 23, 24,
25, 26, 39
North Hall, 26–27, **27**, 30, 32, **33**,
55
Old Armory, 45
Pentacrest, 32, **33**, 34, 35, 135
Physics Building, 56
Political Science, Department of,
37
Preparatory Department, 22, 26
president's office, 23, 25, 31, 37,
58, 69, 71, 114, 115, **124**
recitation rooms, 22, 24, 28, 30, 31
registrar's office, 31
Religion, School of, 41
Schaeffer Hall, 32, **33**
Science Hall, 30, 32, 34
sidewalks, 28
South Hall, 26, **27**, 32, **33**, 39
Speech and Dramatic Art, De-
partment of, 44
students, 25, 41, 44–45, 136
Student Senate, 45, 134
Supreme Court Day, 45, 118

University Hall, 56
water closet, 32, **34,** 35
Writers' Workshop, 134
Zetagathian Society, 25
University of Iowa Foundation, 86

Van Allen, Abigail, 87
Van Brunt, Henry, 32
Vietnam War, 41, 136
Vitols, Arthur, 135

Wadsworth, Albert R., 110
Wagler, Harold, 137
Walpole, Hugh, 43
War between the States, 40

Wells, D. Franklin, 25
Wertsch, Rudolph F., 103–104
White, Charles A., 27
Whiting, Samuel D., 43
Wilder, Thornton, 43
Williamsburg (Virginia), 57
Windrem, William, 18
Woodburn, Mary Ann, 135
World War I, 40, 47
World War II, 40
Wright, Frank Lloyd, 43
Wyrick, Darrell D., xiii

Yewell, George H., 15–16, 146